For my mother

Table of Contents

Foreword

The city of Newark, New Jersey, has had many histories written about it and various of its institutions during the 300 years that have passed since it was settled in 1666. Among these many histories there is a singular omission. None has ever been written about its theater. The present study was undertaken to rectify, in part, this omission.

It has been my intention to investigate and record the professional theater event in Newark from the earliest documented performances through the middle of the nineteenth century. Preliminary investigation revealed a dearth of professional theater activities prior to the construction of a theater building in 1847. At that time, and until shortly after the Civil War, the stock system prevailed. By stock system I mean a system which consisted of a company of players equipped with a repertory of plays and parts which was brought together by contract to a specific management (generally associated with a specific playhouse) for a "season" of a certain number of days or performances. The Civil War marks the break-down of this system and the emergence of the touring company or combination system. It also marks the acceptance of the long-run and "realism." Thus, the period covered by this study finds the stock system at its height and the seeds of change being planted.

Upon establishing the record I found myself with a great body of data about hitherto unknown activities of players. Since this information contributes to our knowledge of the American theater as well as of the cultural life of Newark, it has been my desire to present it in as helpful a manner as possible. Toward this end, I have handled the data in two ways. First, selectively, I present a narrative of the theater in Newark from the first documented performance of a professional player in 1799 to the last effort to establish a stock company in 1867. In this I note those factors which have mitigated for and against the establishment of continuing theater in Newark, the popular players and plays, the buildings which housed performances, the various concerns about the quality of plays and playing, and the relationship of these to the New York and general American theater scenes. Second, inclusively, I present in the form of two appendices all of the recorded performances of every player, every play he or she appeared in, as well as every play that was presented, when and where.

The data was gathered from the periodicals of the period. Through often short-lived publications I was able to cover daily or weekly the entire period, beginning with Wood's Newark Gazette in 1791 to the end. The greater part of the data was found in the pages of the Newark Daily Advertiser, which was active from March 1, 1832, to April 30, 1907. Since the professional theater critic (as we know him today) was not a functioning part of the theater world during the period covered by this study, there was no continuing source of "eye witness" accounts. Thus this data was derived primarily from advertisements, news items or editorials, and letters-to-the-editor. Unfortunately, it appears that some theater companies did not advertise consistently, and perhaps there were others who did not advertise at all. For these otherwise blank periods I was able, in several instances, to find theater playbills or broadsides. It is my hope that additional materials of this nature can be found.

Every effort has been made to make this study accurate and useful both to the student of theater and the general reader. Because of the fugitive and dissembling nature of the material, however, one must assume this story of the Newark theater to be obviously incomplete. Nonetheless, the narrative and the appendices that follow fill a gap in our knowledge of the early American theater and it is hoped that they will serve as a point of departure for future students of the American theater. It is my own intention to continue the story of the Newark theater.

Certainly this study would have been impossible had it not been for the courtesy of the several people who made available to me the resources of their various collections, in particular, The Newark Free Public Library, The New Jersey Historical Society, The Players Club, The New York Public Library, Princeton University Library, and the Rutgers University Library. Many persons, of course, enter into the life of an undertaking such as this, making their various contributions through waiting, encouraging, understanding, listening, and assisting. I should like to thank them all but space doesn't permit listing their names. I should like, however, to express my particular gratitude to the following: Dr. Julia Sabine, who suggested the need for such a study, and Miss Miriam Studley, both of the Newark Free Public Library, for so patiently extending themselves and the facilities of their departments; Mr. Edward Southern Hipp of the Newark News for several articles on theater in Newark which encouraged my discoveries; Dr. Paul Kozelka and Dr. Erling Hunt of Teachers

College, Columbia University, for innumerable suggestions and personal support; my students at Rutgers University in Newark who lived through much of this material with me, in particular: Gail L. Kellstrom, Kenneth Kalis, Vincent J. Mirante, Richard Molicki, and Richard M. Oxman. Finally, I should like to express an incalculable personal debt to my colleague and friend, Dr. Annetta Wood Siegler, former chairman of the Department of Dramatic Art and Speech of Douglass College, Rutgers University, with whose recent, untimely death the world lost not only a great lady, but a sensitive artist-teacher and rare human being.

Chapter I

Of General Background and Particular Setting

For the average theater-goer and theater professional, the American theater has long been located in New York City, while the mark of acceptance (if not standard of excellence) has been Broadway. Since the middle of the nineteenth century, the capital of the American theater has been New York City. Its story has been written many times, most notably by such chroniclers as Ireland, Brown, and Odell. Despite all of this, the full story of the American theater has yet to be written, for this story is as big and varied as the Nation itself. It is the story of local and regional theater activities from Boston to San Francisco, St. Louis to New Orleans, Charleston to Philadelphia, and New York City. The history of the American theater in Newark adds another, heretofore unrecorded, chapter to this ever-expanding narrative.

The history of the American theater reflects the changing face of the Nation, the manners, customs, and business of a people, from settlements and centers of colonial days to those which arose with the expansion to the West. Indeed, the story of the American theater cannot be divorced from those stories which tell of the immigration and migration of human beings, the development and growth of industries and occupations, the birth and death of cities and regional centers. These are the stories of a Nation being born: its comfortable dependency, its struggle for independence, and the growing pains of its search for its own identity. These are paralleled by and reflected in the great study of the American theater.

The first chapter in a complete history of the American theater might be entitled "Introduction, or The British Theater Transplanted in America." This chapter might take us roughly through the American Revolution. Chapter two could take us through the Civil War, and might be entitled "Beginnings, or Efforts Imitative and Native." The story of the Newark theater would begin here. This was the period of the stock company, a group of players who daily performed a repertory of different plays (with songs and dances interspersed for good measure). Chapter two is also, then, "The Age of Stock and the Player." In general, during this time the standards of excellence and models for emulation (if not barely concealed plagiarism among playwrights) were foreign. The native element appears to have been introduced by the players. They devised characters based upon the living types which were emerging in this new Nation: Yankee types such as Jonathan Ploughboy and Solon Shingle, city types such as Mose, the Bowery B'hoy. Often a player would meet with such success in a particular character that he would continue to play the character for years in various, often quickly-scripted, new situations. They were playwrights, of course, making serious efforts with native themes, but the theater did not belong to them. Many changes, however, were coming about.

The seeds of change grow and bear fruit in our next chapter. The long run and the touring company took the place of the daily change of bill of the resident stock company. A growing interest in topical matters gave rise to a

new realism affecting the choice and handling of material by
the playwright as well as its presentation by the players and
scenic artists.   The playwright, director, and critic found
their places.   The disciplines necessary in the creation of a
strong stock company and those further disciplines exacted
earlier by such an actor-manager as the elder J.W. Wallack,
in his insistence upon the ensemble rather than the individual
(long before Saxe-Meiningen), undoubtedly "fathered" the
modern director.   Theater criticism of any systematic nature
had been an unknown commodity.   Whereas the stock company had contended with reviews primarily by way of items or
letters-to-the-editor, the long-run found the professional critic coincident with its emergence.   By that time large theatrical syndicates were absorbing the functions of the independent
theater owner and local producer.   This chapter of our hypo-
thetical history of the American theater brings us to the twentieth century.   It might be entitled simply "The American
Theater Comes of Age."

In not much more than one hundred years following
the War for Independence, the American theater (as opposed
to the foreign theatre in America) might be said to have been
born, have struggled to grow and find itself, and have come
of age.   This span of years-- roughly the nineteenth century--
defies a neat general classification.   Within its confines there
was the flowering both of Romanticism and of Realism.   It
saw the growth of democracy and also the rise of rugged indi-
vidualism.   It knew complacency and self-satisfaction as well
as cynicism and despair.   Perhaps the greatest advances of
the period were made in science.   Perhaps the greatest
changes occurred in the social and economic orders.   The

latter part of the century found everything "new." There was
the "New Geology," "New Biology," "New Psychology," the
"new rich," even the "new woman." It was, of course, an
age of much that was truly new: steamships, railroads, gas
and electricity, telegraphs, telephones, photography, moving
pictures. It was an age that promoted restlessness and one
that saw the passing of many old orders. In the middle of
this age, the city of Newark acquired its first theater, Concert Hall, a hardy construction which existed through many
new orders.

          Although the citizens of Newark had witnessed play
performances given by students and local drama societies
since 1754, and visiting professionals since at least 1799
(according to extant evidence), the actual construction of a
theater for such purposes came late. The little town on
the Passaic River was 181 years old when the first theater
was constructed in 1847. Charleston, South Carolina, although Newark's junior by four years had opened its Dock
Street Theatre in 1736. Williamsburg had a theatre in 1751.
Performances of plays, of course, often predated the construction of actual theaters. The American colonists saw performances (undoubtedly infrequent events) which would be
given in such large or available space as might be found in
their inns or schools. Sometimes a highly temporary make-
shift structure might be erected by a group of "strolling
players." Theater, however, was not a commonly accepted
part of the colonial American cultural scene. The more
general acceptance of theater cannot really be said to have
occurred until the end of the eighteenth century. In 1789
Pennsylvania laws prohibiting theater were repealed. Four

years later Massachusetts and Rhode Island followed suit. In
the early nineteenth century Boston, New York, and Philadelphia emerged as theater centers, with New York taking the
lead in the third decade. During this same time, Newark
also emerged, but as one of the Nation's leading industrial
centers.

      When the first theater was constructed in Newark in
1847, the city was a thriving, culturally inter-mixed industrial center. The Nation's theater center--now New York--
was practically in Newark's front yard, readily accessible as
a result of the strides made in the area of transportation.
It is somewhat ironic that Newark finally acquired a theater
of its own only after the many active theaters of New York
City had become so easily available. It is a commendation
to the citizens of Newark that they were intent upon establishing an independent cultural life for the city at a time when
its cultural needs could have been met with less effort by
New York City. It would have been easier to let New York
absorb the cultural and amusement responsibilities for this
busy industrial center, but instead Concert Hall, Newark's
first theater, persisted, if not always as a cultural center,
certainly as a symbol for Newark's various, continuing efforts
toward self-realization and cultural independence.

      For almost a hundred and fifty years Newark had rest-
ed contentedly, emulating on earth the peace of the Kingdom
of God which its Puritan founders had intended. The citizens
of Newark were industrious and handy with tools. They discovered, as villages grew up around them, that others were
willing to pay money for what they made. Around 1800, almost overnight, the quiet little village became a busy little

town.   Shoemaking, its first industry, engaged nineteen-twen-
tieths of the population who worked for others by 1810.   By
this time, Newark was sending shoes by the wagon loads far
and wide and it had become necessary to hire people from
nearby towns.   The people were now aroused to make and
sell other things.   Coachmaking followed, with the manufacture of coach-lace and saddlery hardware right behind.   Then
came hat making and the manufacture of jewelry.   The construction of the Morris Canal (completed in 1832) and the first
railroad in 1833 not only brought more business to the thriving community, but more laborers as well.   In 1777 Newark
had 141 dwelling houses; in 1833 there were 1,712.   In 1810
there were 6,000 people in the city; in 1833 the population
was estimated at 15,000.   At one time, considerably more
than half of the entire population of Essex county was located
in Newark.   When Newark arose from the quietude of being
a Puritan village, it moved quickly.

By size alone Newark could now support a theater. The
Puritans had disapproved of theater, but Newark was no longer a Puritan village.   Its greatly increased population was
also more diverse.   The Irish settlers starting in the 1820's,
followed by the German, contributed to this diversity.   But
if this new population did not disapprove of theater, they were
apparently much too busy initially to pause to construct one.
They did find time, however, to participate in amateur thea-
tricals.   After 1814, several dramatic societies appeared,
giving their performances for the benefit of a school, church,
or public building.   It is not within the scope of this study to
consider amateur productions.   They present, however, a
slender thread of theatrical continuity extending from the first

recorded performance of a play in Newark in 1754 to the
erection of the first theater in 1847 and beyond.

Newark's first theater, Concert Hall, was constructed
during what might be called the golden age of the stock system, or, perhaps more correctly, the last brilliant period
of a golden era--an era which ended for Newark in 1867.
In 1866, on the two hundredth anniversary of the founding of
Newark, Mr. and Mrs. D. W. Waller leased the theater on
the corner of Market and Harrison (now Halsey) Streets.
They remodeled, redecorated, and rechristened the structure
as Waller's Opera House. They established an outstanding,
well-disciplined stock company, with Mrs. Emma Waller as
directress and leading actress, but it is doubtful that the
public and press fully appreciated the exceptional talent and
quality of production which was afforded them for two seasons
at Waller's Opera House. In December, 1867, the stock
company gave its final performance. Although it could not
have been known at the time, this performance marked also
the end of an era. The rule of stock was over. Gone were
the days of the resident company and visiting star. Not only
in Newark but throughout this young Nation stock companies
of varying quality had established themselves as the amusement centers of their communities. Stock had been king; now
the king was dying.

With the demise of the stock system after the Civil
War, many of the Nation's theater buildings themselves fell
upon bad days. They often became the sometime home of
such diverse events as political rallies, lectures, concerts and
exhibits. Many theaters were simply torn down to make way
for more lucrative enterprises. Of courses, theater struc-

tures were not noted for longevity. Indeed many were des-
troyed by fire after only a few years of existence. In this
respect Newark's Concert Hall was rather exceptional. It
existed as a structure and home of theatrical events for 75
years. As Newark's first theater, it outlived the stock company and the transition into the touring company. After 1880
additional theater structures were increasingly built in the
city, but Newark's first theater continued to be the home of
those "firsts" that emerged in the changing theatrical scene.
The Newark audience was first introduced to vaudeville and
later burlesque on its stage. In the second decade of the
twentieth century, the venerable structure on the corner of
Market and Halsey Streets decided apparently to give up rather than give in to the latest change in the theatrical scene;
the silent film. In 1922 the building was torn down. A
clothing store now stands on the site.

If the very last days of Newark's first theater lacked
the glory of those days in 1847 in which Charlotte Barnes,
J. W. Wallack (the elder), and W. S. Fredericks headed an
outstanding ensemble of players in a repertory drawn primarily from the English dramatists, the theater had, nonetheless, served Newark long and well. For thirty-three years
of its long existence, from 1847 to 1880, through lean as
well as full days, Concert Hall persisted as the Newark
Theatre. Undoubtedly this persistence paved the way for
the competition presented by a flurry of theater construction
which began in 1880. Within six years four new theaters
appeared: the Grand Opera House, the Park, the Academy of
Music, and Miner's Newark Theatre. By 1896 the theatrical
syndicate of Klaw and Erlanger had moved into the city and

added Miner's to their nationwide chain of theaters.   They
were followed within two years by the Shubert boys from
Syracuse who built the Empire Theatre and, a number of
years later, the Sam S. Shubert Theatre.   By the end of
the century Newark had become an active theater center.
The early and solitary persistence of Concert Hall was re-
warded.   But lest we mark the growth in numbers of theaters as success and equate this with quality, we should remember that Concert Hall alone knew the golden years of
stock and housed at least two outstanding, well-disciplined
ensembles which ruled its boards with the sceptre of royalty.
In an age of the actor, the solitary persistence of Concert
Hall made it possible for the citizens of Newark to see such
theatrical crowned heads and royalty as Augustus A. Addams,
Charlotte M. S. Barnes, Edwin Booth, F. S. Chanfrau, E. S.
Conner, Lotta Crabtree, Pauline Cushman, E. L. Davenport,
Rose Eytinge, W. S. Fredericks, Kate Fisher, James A.
Hearne, Matilda Heron, "Yankee" Hill, Mr. and Mrs. G. C.
Howard, Fanny Janauschek, Lola Montez, Ristori, J. S. Sils-
bee, J. W. Wallack (the elder), Emma Waller, and Mr. and
Mrs. Barney Williams, to name a few.

The chronicle that follows describes the various for-
tunes of the actors.   It is divided into periods, each of which
presents the efforts of actor-managers to establish a permanent stock company in Newark.   The first chapter is dominated by players who were trained in the English (or intellectual) tradition.   Diversity and a variety of efforts keynotes
Chapter Two.   In Chapter Three, the theater is dominated by
adventure and spectacle.   Chapter Four records the last efforts to establish a repertory of English and more intellec-

tual plays, while accepting the demands for the lighter, popular works. In many respects, Concert Hall is the real
hero of this chronicle, but the actors who passed across its
stage made theater an important part of the cultural life of
Newark. The story of their efforts in Newark adds another
chapter to the total story of the American theater.

Chapter II

Of Pioneers and a Golden Reign

Not unlike other communities in the Garden State, Newark, from its settling in 1666 through the eighteenth century, found its chief support in agriculture. Patrick Falconer, an early settler in New Jersey, wrote to Morris Trent from "Elizabeth Town in East Jersey" on October 28, 1684, and had nothing but good words for New Jersey. He found it "a good Countrey for men who resolve to be laborious, [but] not a Countrey for idle people."[1] Judging from the sometime spelling of its early name The Town of New Work was not settled by people who intended to be idle. By the end of the eighteenth century candlemaking, jewelry manufacture, grist mills, and saw mills all contributed to local prosperity. The city was noted, however, for its cider and whiskey distilling as well as for the making of carriages of all sorts. In the first part of the nineteenth century the manufacture of men's and women's shoes alone occupied one-third of the inhabitants and hat manufacturing was a promising infant industry. The increasingly busy brownstone quarries and iron foundries added to the industrial activity.[2]

New Work and Things Cultural

Nor were the citizens of New Work idle in their concern with education. In 1746 the College of New Jersey began operation in combination with the classical school estab-

21

lished by the Presbyterian minister, Rev. Aaron Burr.[3]
The institution which was to become Princeton University, although founded in Elizabeth, moved its first classes to Newark.   The college remained in Newark eight years before
eventually finding its present, more centrally-located home.
In 1787 the Orange Academy began operation under the super-
vision of the Orange Dale Church.   Our first records of play
performances in Newark are of those productions given by
students.   In 1754 two students of the College of New Jersey
"acted Tamerlane and Bajazet, etc."[4] On July 4, 1791, for
"a second time," the students of the Orange Academy presented "a modern comedy" entitled Maccasophos.[5]

        In 1791 Newark's first newspaper, Woods's Newark
Gazette, began operation.   In the pages of the Gazette we
note a growing concern for the cultural life of Newark, the
reward for accomplishment by the "laborious."   Although our
early settlers might have considered it idleness, Tristram,
writing to Mr. Woods on December 22, 1791, made an eloquent plea for theaters as places for winter amusement. He
informed Mr. Woods and his readers that "the theatres now
open their doors as pleasant retreats wherein we may enter,
and forgetting a while the gloom of nature, and the gloom of
our minds, pass agreeably a few tedious hours; and have our
hearts softened into a sweet kind of melancholy or meliorated
with lightsome mirth . . . ."[6]

        Despite Tristram's plea for an interest in things
cultural, more than half a century passed before Newark
acquired its first theater building.   Colonial puritanism,
which had governed the town on the Passaic river from its
early days, was weakened twice: first by the large immigra-

tion of Irish in the 1830's and later by the large German
immigration of the late 1840's.[7] Then the little town became an industrial center. But when the puritanical res-
trictions which had long delayed the construction of a theater
were broken and Newark could respond to an increasing need
for places of amusement, other factors emerged which res-
tricted the cultural growth of the city. New York, so very
close, was already established as an amusement center. It
offered diversification and choice. The boards of Concert
Hall, Newark's first theater, had to present that which would
satisfy the desires of a cultural and social inter-mixture. In
effect, one theater in Newark had to compete with the various
specialized appeals and standards of excellence of the established houses and companies of New York. In so doing,
Concert Hall presented Newark with that diversification
which was characteristic of the American stage in New York.
In the last decade of the eighteenth century, however, cultural-
minded Newarkers combined amusement with edification when
they attended the various exercises given by the students at
Orange Academy.

First Recorded Professionals, 1799

The Orange Academy (often referred to at this time
as Newark Academy) also housed the first recorded professional performance of a play in Newark On August 6, 1799,
an advertisement in the Newark Gazette announced "theatre
by permission" to the ladies and gentlemen of Newark and
its vicinity. On the next evening, "at a commodious room
in Newark Academy will be presented, (by way of Prelude)
a Moral Lesson extracted from Mrs. Thrale's Three Warn-

ings or Death an Unwelcomed Visitor, to be recited by Mr.
Bates." This was followed by a dramatic entertainment,
titled, No Song No Supper and the farce, The Mock Doctor
or The Dum Lady Cured [sic] with Mrs. Seymour. She and
Mr. Bates were members of Dunlap's company in New York.
William Dunlap, from Perth Amboy, New Jersey, had opened
the Park Theatre in New York the year before. His season
had closed for the summer on July 4, 1799. [8] Of his company, Mrs. Seymour, at any rate, spent part of her summer
in Newark.

On August 20 another advertisement appeared in the
Newark Gazette announcing "A Moral Lesson for Youth Called
George Barnwell," again with Mrs. Seymour, to be given the
next day and on the following "Mondays, Wednesdays, and
Fridays." No records exist to support conjecture as to how
many, if any, Monday, Wednesday and Friday performances
took place. We know only that the Ball (could this be a
benefit?) for Mrs. Seymour which was "advertised for Friday
last" was postponed until the next Friday, October 4. It was
to take place in the Long Room of Mr. Tuttle's Tavern. [9]

At this time and for several decades to follow, Newark
appeared to be wanting in amusements in general and culture
in particular, but this conclusion is a matter of definition.
As Foster R. Dulles informs us: "In the opening decades of
the nineteenth century, American people throughout the east-
ern parts of the country were enjoying very much the same
recreations as they had in colonial days."[10] These were
singled out by Timothy Dwight, about 1821, as "visiting,
dancing, music, conversation, walking, riding, sailing, shoot-
ing at a mark, draughts, chess, and unhappily in some of

the larger towns, cards and dramatic exhibitions."[11] Happily
for Mr. Dwight but unhappily for our record of theater, Newark (according to extant evidence) was not to be visited again
by a professional player until a company of players arrived
in 1832.

Professional Company at Mansion House, 1832

At the solicitations of "many respectable citizens,"
Messrs. Thorne and Mestayer ("late of the Bowery and Richmond Hill Theatres") announced on May 7, 1832, that they
had "gone to the expense of fitting up the Hall at the Mansion
House in a neat and appropriate style, with new scenery,
dresses, decorations, etc. [with] the Company comprising
experienced and talented actors and actresses" from the Albany, Southern, and West India Theatres in addition to the
two already mentioned. Their season extended from May 8 to
May 19 with the "celebrated American Tragedian," Mr. A.
Addams joining the company on the 14th. Other than those
mentioned the company consisted of Messrs. Lennox, Meer,
Janvia, Chipp, Wray and Mesdames Thorne, Mestayer, Belcour, and Miss Smith. The season included Wandering Boys,
Spoil'd Child, the melodrama currently "playing to crowded
houses in New York" entitled Victorine or I'll Sleep on It,
Stranger or Misanthropy and Repentence, Fortune's Frolic,
Spectre Bridegroom, Turnpike Gate, Rendezvous, and with
Mr. Addams, Damon and Pythias, Iron Chest, Richard III or
The Battle of Bosworth Field, Sheridan's version of Pizzaro
or The Death of Rolla, Act III of Othello, Tom and Jerry,
and Robber's Wife along with various other afterpieces.[12]

Mr. Augustus Addams was undoubtedly the most dis-
tinguished member of the company which, other than for Mr.

Janvia, "late of the Southern Theatres," was drawn most
recently from the membership of the Richmond Hill Theatre
in New York City. [13]   On April 30 the Richmond Hill ended
a season which has been characterized by Odell as having "a
poor company, undistinguished stars (Mrs. Duff excepted),
a remarkable succession of amateur first appearances, and
only one vital new play--Victorine."[14]   One cannot say whether a lack of distinction carried over to the Newark season.
Judging, however, from the often confusing early theatrical
records, it would appear that many members of this company led busy professional lives and were in demand.   Lennox
and Mrs. Mestayer, for example, were among those announced
as appearing exclusively at the Bowery for the spring, 1832,
season.   How Lennox managed, if he did, to be at the Bowery
and Richmond Hill is not known.   Mr. Thorne had become
proprietor of the Chatham on May 4, 1831, from which position he apparently joined the Richmond Hill company in
November.   Prior to that he had been a member of the
Bowery where, for example, he had undertaken Iago to the
Othello of Mr. A. Addams.   There he had also appeared
with Mrs. French, the former Miss Anna Mestayer, who was
to become Mrs. Thorne. [15]

        Whatever may have been the quality of the Thorne-
Mestayer season, they nonetheless brought to Newark a
sampling of the current theatrical fare then existing in New
York, including the "vital new play" Victorine, with the title
role undoubtedly performed by Miss Smith who had essayed
it in the original Richmond Hill production.   Fifteen years
were to pass, however, before Newark was to be given another sampling of a professional theater season, unless one

counts the brief docking, in 1845, of a showboat.

The City of Newark Emerges

Newark was passing rapidly from a country town into
a thriving industrial center. In 1835, when Pierson published his first City Directory, the population was 18,201. The
next year, 1836, the city census discovered 19,732, a decided
increase from the 8,017 of ten years earlier. The coachmaking and hatting industries drew more and more Irish settlers. River traffic on the Passaic became so great that
Congress had named Newark a port of entry by 1833. In
1835 the New Jersey Railroad and Transportation Company
began operations. That and the building of the Morris Canal
not only increased the laboring population but contributed toward making Newark New Jersey's leading industrial center.[16]
In 1836 Newark was incorporated as a city and became, so
Atkinson (Newark's early historian) tells us, "the mould of
fashion, the observed of all observers among neighboring
towns." Newark's citizens were cited for "energy and enter-
prize . . . an incentive to ambition, and an example for imi-
tation."[17]

The erection of new buildings paralleled the city's
growth in population. The Long Rooms and Saloons of the
early inns and hotels were increasingly inadequate for the
various public meetings, socials, and concerts. In the early
1840's Newark had several fine public halls, but there was
still a need for a less versatile building, designed especially
for theatrical performance. This need led eventually to the
construction, by 1847, of Concert Hall, which, despite its
name, was designed for and almost immediately taken over

by theater people.

The First Theater: Concert Hall, 1847

An observer in the Newark Daily Advertiser for February 3, 1847, pronounced Concert Hall "decidedly the most
elegant public room in the city. It has commodious pews
and a fine private gallery where the exquisite may find a safe
retreat from the crowd below; and all so well arranged that
every one, even the hindermost, may have a complete view
of the stage . . . . The impression on entering the room is
one of beauty, and the long row of Corinthian columns com-
bine a wild grandeur and produce an effect truly imposing."[18]
The "room" was 50 feet wide and 110 feet long. Four rows
of permanent seats with backs fronted the stage. The floor
of the house rose gradually from the stage to the entrance,
above which was the gallery also as wide as the room. The
building was lighted with gas and was the first public structure in Newark to be so. [19] The Newark Gaslight Company
had begun manufacturing on Christmas Day, 1846. [20]

The building stood on the corner of Market and Harrison Streets. On the ground floor, opening onto Market
Street, the equipment of the Newark Volunteer Firemen was
housed. Behind were the stables. The theater was on the
second floor of the three-storied structure. (Six years later,
however, following the removal of the stables, it was dropped
to the first floor.) The stage of the theatre was 22 feet by
24 and "fitted up with reference to convenience and taste."[21]
This suggests a proscenium opening of 22 feet. If so, approximately 14 feet of wing space was provided for on either
side of the stage (unless dressing rooms were on the side
rather than at the back, above or below). With 24 feet of

depth, the stage of Concert Hall could handle changing scenic effects with ease.   Unfortunately no visual records exist to aid us in our reconstruction of Newark's first building de- signed for the performance of legitimate theater.   A vocal touring group had no hesitation in speaking of its sound and comfort, which they pronounced "one of the very best in the country. "[22]   Whatever its facilities, Concert Hall soon at- tracted some of the finest theater artists of the day and New- ark was to know, though briefly, a reign of gold.

First Stock Company at Concert Hall

A simple statement tucked into a page of heterogeneous advertisements and announcements called the attention of the readers of the Newark Daily Advertiser of April 8, 1847, to a "Dramatic Festival (for a few nights only), under the mana- gement of Sullivan and Miller. "   It was to take place in the recently constructed Concert Hall, which for the first two months of its existence had served for benefits (the Firemen and the "starving in Ireland, " among others), bringing New- arkers such entertainment as that provided by The Allegha- nians and Christy's Far Famed and Original Band of Ethio- pian Minstrels.   Now Messrs. Sullivan and Miller announced that Concert Hall "has been fitted up in a neat and appro- priate manner, with elegant scenery and appointments, "[23] and thus Concert Hall became Newark's first legitimate theater.

The company for the Dramatic Festival consisted of Mr. William S. Fredericks, Mrs. Watts, Mrs. Harrison, and Miss LaForest[24] who had been members of the short- lived New York Opera House venture which had probably end- ed before April. [25]   The Dramatic Festival advertisement

made no mention, however, of that venture, but, rather, listed Mr. Fredericks and Mrs. Harrison as from the Park
Theatre and Mrs. Watts from the Olympic. Others listed for
the Newark company were Mrs. Frary, the managers, Sullivan and Miller, and Messrs. Brandon, King, Herbert, Stafford and Vanstavoren. [26]

     The opening production was Tobin's The Honeymoon
(sometimes listed as Honey Moon) or How to Rule a Wife,
with Irish Tutor as the afterpiece. [27] The next day, the local
reviewer commended the performers of the opening night as
having "fully justified all that might have been expected from
them, " and singled out Mr. Fredericks as having sustained
his part "in a most able manner, fully justifying his high reputation. "[28] The second night brought competition from "Yankee" Hill who was presenting a program of his characterizations that evening only at Washington Hall, [29] and ten days
and seven performances later, the Dramatic Festival was
replaced on the Concert Hall stage by the return of Christy's
Minstrels, which remained for five performances. [30]

     Prior to the return of Christy's Minstrels, however,
Mr. H. P. Grattan (also of the defunct New York Opera
House) and the celebrated "Jim Crow" Rice joined the Newark
company and citizens saw The Stranger, Knowles' The Wife,
The Dumb Belle, Lady of Lyons, and Othello, as well as Mr.
Rice's "burlesque opera, " Otello, Jumbo Jim, The Virginian
Mummy, and The Foreign Prince or Jim Crow in London.
Mr. Rice's benefit on Saturday, April 17, 1847, was the last
day "of the present season. "[31]

The Golden Reign

The brief essay into the cultural climate of Newark exemplified by the Dramatic Festival suggests there may have been hope for the establishment of a stock company, or perhaps dogged determination accounts for the announcement of a "new season" at Concert Hall in less than three weeks after the close of the first.[32] Messrs. Sullivan and Miller had withdrawn from the management. Messrs. Herbert and Millar joined as management and lessees of the theater. For the next few months the "people" of Newark were entertained by "royalty" and Concert Hall was the great democratic meeting place. Outstanding performers, dedicated to the best of the stock system--ensemble playing--presented a repertory of the best plays. At Concert Hall an ideal was given expression: a democracy may be culturally a nation, not of common men, but of aristocrats. Three figures initially exemplify this idea: Miss Charlotte Barnes, who was originally engaged for only the first five performances of the new season, Mr. J. W. Wallack (the elder), and Mr. William S. Fredericks.

The Queen: Charlotte Barnes

Miss Barnes, "owing to severe indisposition," was prevented from appearing as scheduled for the first three nights of the new season. Charles the II'd [sic] apparently opened the new season on May 4, 1847, with Mr. H. R. Hunt in the title role. The next evening, Mr. Nickinson made his first appearance in Newark in Monsieur Jaques [sic]. On May 6, Miss Barnes, then recovered, appeared as The

Youthful Queen or Christina of Sweden, following it the next
night with Lady of Lyons. Mr. William Henry Herbert, Newark author who wrote under the name of Frank Forester,
came to the Market Street theater from his farm-estate, The
Pines, to see Lady of Lyons. Of this experience he reported:

> I was one of the audience which listened last
> evening to the performance of the "Lady of
> Lyons" with the highest pleasure, and am grati-
> fied that we have now an opportunity to listen to
> the readings of English Dramatists free from
> the usual evils which attend theatrical represen-
> tations. The representation of Pauline last
> evening by Miss Charlotte Barnes was indeed
> a beautiful piece of acting throughout. The true
> secret of her success lies in the soul which she
> throws in her delineation of character, the
> passionate thoughts that well up as it were from
> the deep fountain of a noble heart: and she
> peculiarly personified the sentiment expressed . . . [33]

An acquaintance with the English dramatists and an insight into the "secret" of success in performance were very
much within the scope of Miss Barnes' professional life. The
daughter of Mr. and Mrs. John Barnes, highly esteemed actors who had been recruited from London in 1816 for the ail-
ing Park Theatre in New York,[34] Miss Barnes had been "edu-
cated for the stage," Ireland informs us. As an actress,
however, she never, in New York at any rate, seemed to
"gain a permanent footing on the boards."[35] In Newark, to
the contrary, she became "the people's favorite."

Miss Barnes was also a playwright. Her play Octavia
Bragaldi was first produced at J. W. Wallack's National Theatre, New York, on November 9, 1837, with Miss Barnes herself acting Octavia. As a practicing lady playwright, Charlotte Barnes, with Octavia Bragaldi, predated Anna Cora Mowatt

and Fashion by some eight years. In 1847, at least four
plays by Miss Barnes already had been presented in America
or England: The Captive; The Forest Princess; La Fitte, The
Pirate of the Gulf; and Octavia Bragaldi. By the next year,
her volume Plays, Prose, and Poetry was published in Philadelphia, and another play, A Night of Expectations, was presented in Chicago, with Charlotte Corday yet to come.[36]

Newark saw Miss Barnes several times in 1847 in her
play, The Captive or A Tragic Scene in a Private Mad
House.[37] (Later, in 1848 and 1849, she appeared in The
Forest Princess and Octavia Bragaldi.) Otherwise her repertoire contained the aforementioned The Youthful Queen,
Lady of Lyons, J. S. Knowles' The Hunchback and The
Stranger, the Rev. H. H. Milman's Fazio or The Italian
Wife, and The Belle's Stratagem, generally with the support
of Mr. Fredericks and Mr. Nickinson. On May 17, Mr.
Nickinson's benefit brought Miss Anna Cruise to Concert Hall
in A Roland for an Oliver. Mr. Nickinson was leaving Newark, a newspaper item observed, for a two week engagement
in Baltimore, after which he planned to return.[38]

With Court

On May 18, the management announced in the Advertiser "the first appearance in Newark of the celebrated Mr.
Wallack [the elder] and (at considerable expense) the valuable
aid of the popular and talented favorite, Miss Charlotte
Barnes," making her third re-engagement with the Newark
company. Little more than a month earlier, Mr. Wallack
had made his first appearance in New York at the Park after
an absence in England of three years.[39] With the continuing

assistance of Mr. Fredericks, the management could say with
justifiable pride that they were "presenting a cast of characters equal to any establishment in the United States."[40]

In its leading actors, Concert Hall had three whose
traditions were rooted in those of New York's Park Theatre.
All three--Barnes, Wallack, and Fredericks--had made their
American debuts there. Only Miss Barnes was native; the
gentlemen had been imported from London and Dublin respectively. All three had worked together before and could be
said to represent the best of the English tradition and training. Ten years earlier (1837), Wallack had made his first
essay into management, thus beginning a career that was to
make him a major influence on the American theater. He
leased the National Theatre in New York and in his productions there (which had included Miss Barnes' Octavia Bragaldi) set a new standard. He insisted upon "an absolute perfection of ensemble playing" and the "achievement of a total
. . . dramatic effect to which the individual performance of
actors were subordinated."[41] It is not difficult to believe
that the Newark theater-goer discovered at Concert Hall "the
legitimate drama . . . exhibited in a style not to be sur-
passed in this country."[42]

The combination of Wallack, Barnes, and Fredericks
performed at Concert Hall from May 18 to June 1. During
this time, Mr. Wallack missed one performance because of
an indisposition, and a storm canceled another performance.
Nonetheless, during this time, Newarkers saw The Merchant
of Venice, Othello, Catharine and Petruchio, Hamlet by
Shakespeare; and Ernestine or Which Is My Cousin, an "entirely new comedy" as acted by Mr. Wallack originally in

London, and a few weeks earlier in New York. [43]

In the June 3rd edition of the Newark Daily Advertiser Messrs. Herbert and Millar announced with pleasure
the "justly celebrated . . . only true delineator of . . .
genuine Yankee character, Mr. J. S. Silsbee," making his
first appearance in Newark. Supported by Mr. Phillips and
Mr. and Mrs. Charles Howard, Mr. Silsbee presented
Yankee Land; The American Farmers or The Forest Rose;
The Wool Pedlar; and, for his benefit on June 7, "the first
and only time here, the entire new prize drama (written expressly for Mr. Silsbee) from the sketches of the celebrated
Judge Halliburton, entitled Sam Slick, The Clock Maker."[44]
Mr. Silsbee made his first New York appearance as a star
at the New Chatham in 1843. As a Yankee character he was
comparable to Marble and Hill. A London critic in Tallis
Magazine said that his style was considerably different from
either of the others, "and is indeed so far peculiar that it
may be said to form a new and original school."[45] For the
local commentator, however, it was sufficient to note that
Mr. Silsbee's "capital imitations . . . are producing much
amusement."[46]

Hopes must have been high those first months. Professional theater in Newark seemed to have found a home in
the structure on the corner of Market and Harrison Streets.
Those associated with the enterprise were ladies and gentlemen of their profession, a not unimportant consideration. A
gentleman of the city, writing to The Temperance Advocate,
took "great pleasure in being able to say that I have seen
nothing produced which was at all calculated to vitiate the
appetite, or demoralize the mind--nothing I should be afraid

that my wife or my daughters should witness." The managers, Messrs. Millar and Herbert, he commended as "two
gentlemen of excellent character and gentlemanly deport-
ment."[47] Trouble was brewing behind the scenes, however,
which was to throw some doubt upon this commendation.

Conflict in The Counting House
The benefit of Mr. W. J. L. Millar was announced
for June 9, for which occasion Miss Barnes and Mr. Fredericks returned. Rowe's tragedy of Jane Shore or The Unhappy Favorite was to be the main attraction, with Miss
Barnes' The Captive as the after-piece. It did not take
place. The following day, in place of the regular advertisement, two Newark newspapers printed a notice "To the
Public" signed by Messrs. William S. Fredericks, H. B.
Hunt, Charles D. S. Howard, H. N. Sprague, and Mrs.
Amelia Harrison, followed by "A Card" from Mr. Hunt. The
signers of the public notice took their action "in justice to a
slandered man," Mr. Millar, against whom "no charge of
dishonesty or unfairness can be with justice brought," because "he never had at any time the least control over the
funds received."[48] Apparently someone had misappropriated,
if not absconded with, the funds. Mr. Herbert was sus-
piciously conspicuous by his absence.

Whatever trouble had been brewing behind the scenes
had apparently boiled over publicly on the evening of Mr.
Silsbee's benefit (June 7). An article in The Temperance
Advocate informs us of what was

> well known to those who were present . . . that
> Mr. Charles D. S. Howard refused to play him-
> self, or allow his wife to do so, because they

had not received the salary stipulated to be
paid them by the Managers, Messrs. Millar
and Herbert.   Mr. Howard was very much
excited while addressing the audience, and
consequently, he indulged in language entirely unbecoming, including Mr. Millar in his
denunciations, while that gentleman was
entirely innocent of any dishonest intentions
towards him or any other person connected
with the establishment.   Mr. Howard has
since discovered that he had reproached an
individual who did not deserve it, and like
a true gentleman he confesses his fault in
the above notice.

Two days after Mr. Howard's public display, however, the
pot was still boiling over publicly.

Wednesday evening was appointed by Mr. Millar
for his benefit; and being entirely satisfied with
the management of Mr. M. during her engagement, Charlotte Barnes addressed him in excellent letter, expressing her willingness (though
at great inconvenience to herself), to perform
at said benefit. -- She was accordingly cast for
the splendid character of "Jane Shore" and "The
Captive."   She was promptly on the spot at
the time appointed -- attended rehearsal in the
afternoon, and in the evening appeared in her
piece, and dressed for the character of Jane
Shore.   The following individuals all pledged
themselves at the rehearsal that they would
perform the parts assigned them, viz, Messrs.
Phelps, Sprague, Hield, Warwick, Brian,
Dunlan, and also Mrs. Harrison.   Quite a respectable audience assembled at the Hall to witness the performances; but to their everlasting
disgrace be it spoken, Messrs. Hield, Phelps,
Warwick, and Brian violated their solemn
pledge, and obstinately refused to assist in the
performance, thereby not only basely insulting
the people's favorite, Miss Barnes, but the
people also, who were present. [49]

Of Benefits and Business

Certainly such actions, for whatever justifications, constituted a public insult for the person for whom the benefit was designed, and, as the writer points out further, it deprived him of the opportunity and "power to liquidate the claims" against him. [50] The benefit was an important feature in the economic system of the theater from the beginning of the nineteenth century until after the Civil War. Although it was a custom more typically afforded the actor, managers very often gave themselves benefits. This was sometimes an indication that the current season had not been financially successful. Under the stock system, the manager, or managers as was often the case, assumed all of the risk and responsibility. [51] The manager owned all of the production necessities (other than costumes which the actor generally furnished) such as settings and properties, and either owned or leased the theater. As Bernheim points out, "the manager hired the actors on weekly salary, plus benefits, was responsible for all expenses and entitled to all profits." [52]

The practice of the benefit was generally limited to leading members of the resident stock company and visiting stars. Whereas the member of the company was permitted one or more benefits for the season, the visitor was given one at the close of his engagement and each successive re-engagement. The actor taking a benefit was entitled to all the receipts of that performance, which was certainly an incentive for developing a following. [53] On the other hand, the public was often quite partisan toward its favorites. New York's Astor Place Riot in 1848 was a demonstration of the extremes of such partisanship.

One can only conjecture as to the problems presented
to Mr. Millar through the apparent loss of management funds
as well as by the ill-fated opportunity to recoup. It is possible that Mr. Hunt was also as important as a benefactor
as he was as an actor member of the company. His "Card"
of June 10 announced a benefit for himself and assured those
who might be "disposed to patronize the proposed entertainment at Concert Hall on Friday evening" that they would not
be disappointed. The performance would positively take place
with Mr. G. Barrett ("who has in the kindest manner volun-
teered his services for this occasion"), Mr. Fredericks, Mr.
and Mrs. Howard (the former Rosina Shaw), and Mr. Chubb,
the leader of the Park Theatre, "together with the principal
members of the orchestra of that theatre," and Mrs. Harrison.[54] One may hope that Mr. Hunt's benefit not only took
place but was well attended. However that may have been,
the current management had obviously ended and Concert Hall
did not advertise further productions for the next few days.
Thus the idealistic efforts of the company of theater artists
("equal to any establishment in the United States") presenting
the English legitimate drama ("in a style not to be sur-
passed") suffered a realistic setback.

Inter Regnum: Mr. Nickinson

Whatever hope for the establishment of legitimate
theater in Newark that may have been dashed by the "bank-
ruptcy" of Herbert and Millar, should have been revived by
an announcement in the Advertiser on Wednesday, June 16,
1847. Mr. Nickinson, not unlike the hero in a melodrama,
had returned from his engagement in Baltimore, and now

"respectfully announces to citizens of Newark and its vicini-
ties that he has leased [Concert Hall] and intends opening it
for the production of light musical and dramatic entertainments in the style of Mitchell's Olympic, N.Y." He intended to preclude the financial debacle of the previous management by taking his cue from William Mitchell whose New York
Olympic Theatre was successful as the home of light popular
fare.

At this time, according to Coad and Mims, the New
York theaters tended "toward specialization in one particular
type of entertainment calculated to appeal to the tastes of its
own clientele."[55] Mitchell's Olympic specialized in burlet-
tas (short comic pieces consisting of recitative and singing),
extravaganzas, farces (which were Mitchell's own specialty),
and satires or burlesques on practically all topics of public
interest, fashions, fads, as well as current theater productions. According to Odell, the Olympic was the theater "toward which the less intellectual of the playgoers yearned."[56]
Mitchell had rented the relatively new Olympic during the
economic depression that had followed the financial panic of
1837. He had been a member of J. W. Wallack's company
and, as Lloyd Morris points out, he adopted Wallack's poli-
cies "of excellence in stagecraft and of having a strong stock
company . . . . In the existing hard times, he believed that
only the lightest theatrical fare, offered at the lowest possible prices, would attract a public beset by financial
troubles." From its opening in December, 1839, and for
the next ten years, Mitchell's Olympic was one of the most
successful theaters in the country.[57] Mr. Nickinson had
been a popular member of that company for several

seasons. In emulating the "style of Mitchell's Olympic," he undoubtedly hoped also to achieve a similar success. Would the new specialization of Concert Hall, with its less intellectual appeals, find a new audience?

As lessee and manager, Mr. Nickinson made Concert Hall, however, briefly, the continuing home of legitimate theater in Newark, despite a certain apathy on the part of the public as the spring turned into summer. From June 17 to July 12, Newark saw such performers as Messrs. Chanfrau, (of whom we shall hear more), Wm. Conover, Blecker, J. W. Clarke, J. W. Roberts, Sprague, Harrison, Nickinson, Miss Wheeler, Miss Nickinson, Master F. Drew, the Misses Kate (aged 9 years) and Susan Dennin (aged 11 years), from Mitchell's Olympic or the Park Theatre. Also, the "celebrated Irish comedian," Mr. Barney Williams,[58] who will appear many times before the end of this narrative. After 1850, however, it will be the celebrated Mr. and Mrs. Barney Williams upon whom history focuses.

Within two weeks of the opening production, a somewhat lengthy announcement appeared in the Advertiser, calling attention to "the talented corps of performers, . . . the very capable management of Mr. Nickinson . . . well known to the public as a gentleman and a sterling actor," as well as to the obviation of anything offensive during performances, such as the sale of intoxicating drinks, "a feature which attends like places of amusement in a neighboring city."[59] It is not known to what extent the public responded to this announcement, nor to what extent they supported the theater at Concert Hall, but apparently whatever support was given was not enough to warrant Mr. Nickinson carrying the season

beyond Mr. Chanfrau's benefit on July 12.   In closing Concert
Hall, Mr. Nickinson thanked those friends in Newark who had
supported him, "notwithstanding the excessive heat which com-
pelled him to close the establishment until a more genial
season . . . ."[60]

The Court Reconvenes

Although not for Mr. Nickinson, a "more genial season" apparently appeared within a fortnight.   On July 24 the
public was "respectfully informed that Concert Hall will open
for a short season of ten nights, with almost an entirely new
company . . . ."   On July 27, Mr. Fredericks (serving as
Stage Manager also) and Miss Charlotte Barnes opened the
"short season" with Romeo and Juliet, which was announced
as being acted in Newark for the first time.   They were joined by Mr. Stark (in his first Newark appearance) who played
Romeo to Miss Barnes' Juliet, with Mr. Fredericks enacting
Mercutio. [61]

With the return of Miss Barnes and Mr. Fredericks
we can expect and find a return to what we have called the
English (or intellectual) tradition, a tradition strikingly associated with New York's Park Theatre.   The several theaters of New York permitted the playgoer a choice of fare,
but along with this came social distinctions, and snob appeals
to things English as well as snob appeals to things American.
With only one theater the Newark playgoer had to rely upon
the choice of the various managements for his theatrical fare.
The differences in the appeals of the season of Nickinson and
that of Barnes and Fredericks very likely reflect efforts to
"find" the Newark audience.   Be that as it may, the end of

July would not seem to be a good month to find any audience.
Nonetheless, at the end of July "the people's favorite" returned to Newark and brought with her a return to the English,
or perhaps more appropriately, intellectual tradition.

For the second evening (July 28) of the Barnes-Fredericks season Newarkers were offered Otway's Venice Preserved or A Plot Discovered, followed by The Rendezvous.
For the third evening the advertisement for Concert Hall announced a group of amateurs from New York who were
making their first and only appearance in Newark.   Their
performance was to commence with Damon and Pythias or
A Test of Friendship.   It included the farces Perfection, and
The Married Rake. [62]   Several of the amateurs remained
with the Concert Hall company.

The company continued the season with Miss Barnes,
Fredericks, Stark, Mrs. Harrison, and Mr. Augustus A.
Addams, who was brought back to Newark for one evening.
On August 5 they presented Pizarro or The Spaniards in
Peru, with Mr. Stark, Miss Barnes, and Mrs. Harrison.
For the benefit of Mrs. Harrison on August 6, Mr. Augus-
tus A. Addams made his "first and only appearance" in Iron
Chest or The Force of Conscience with Mrs. Harrison, and
concluded with the farce of The Young Widow.   Honeymoon,
with Mr. Fredericks and Miss Barnes, was presented on
August 7.   It was followed with Miss Barnes' own "Thrilling
Piece," The Captive or A Scene in a Private Madhouse. [63]
Although this performance was also to be the farewell benefit of Mr. Fredericks, he continued to appear for awhile
(perhaps somewhat to his chagrin) with the theater he had
been so much a part of from its first performance in April.

The Queen Abdicates

On Monday evening, August 9, the celebrated tragedy
of Virginius or The Roman Father by Knowles was announced
for the first and only time in Newark. Mr. Fredericks appeared as Virginius, Mr. Stark as Icilius, and Miss Barnes
as Virginia. This was followed by the comedietta Is He
Jealous? with Mr. Stark and Miss Barnes. Also in the Advertiser of that day was an article which called attention to
a complimentary benefit production of Hamlet to be given by
Miss Barnes on August 12.

> It is hoped that a due appreciation of her
> chaste and beautiful performances will fill
> the hall in every part. Difficult as has been
> the range of characters sustained by her,
> raising the finest efforts of human genius and
> the most delicate delineations of human char-
> acter, she has yet shown herself equal to
> them all and displayed a most rare combina-
> tion of histrionic talent. Upon the occasion
> of her benefit she will sustain the part of
> Hamlet in that Masterpiece of human genius
> and we doubt not that the performance will
> compare favorably with the masterly repre-
> sentation of the philosophic Dane which we
> have recently witnessed. It is an arduous
> undertaking, but her readings of this play
> have been admired wherever heard and the
> following extract from the notice of Miss
> Barnes in the Blackburn-Lanchester Stand-
> ard attests the favorable opinions which her
> performance in this part elicited from England.

The Blackburn-Lanchester [England] Standard, which this
writer quoted, said:

> Friday evening Miss Barnes took her benefit
> in a crowded house where ample testimony
> was given to her merits. On this occasion,
> she selected HAMLET to appear in, sustaining

the principle character herself. In face and
appearance Miss Barnes was quite a poetical
embodiment of Shakespeare's sublime creation.
And she has so much natural energy tempered
with judgement, plays with so much a finish
and has so carefully studied the intent of the
great author, that there was a freshness and a
beauty about the representation, it would be
difficult under similar circumstances to parallel.
We remember to have seen one female only,
Mrs. West, a metropolitan actress of at one
time considerable celebrity, in this character.
And though she brought double the experience
of Miss Barnes to bear upon this task, she
failed to produce half the effect of this young
lady. Miss Barnes was warmly and frequently
applauded during the performance and at the
falling of the curtain was loudly called for when
she received several additional and hearty rounds
of applause.

The Newark writer went on to say:

This is indeed praise of an unqualified nature
but we are satisfied that her delineation of this
character will exhibit the fine and delicate touches
of that mastermind whose power is ever present
in the magnificent creations of his genuis. We
trust that not another word is necessary to call
out with such an expression of popular feeling
as will testify that we appreciate merit in the
higher walks of dramatic excellence. [64]

Farewell Performance

Miss Barnes, in her farewell to Newark, was supported by Mr. Chanfrau as Laertes, Mr. Cooper as Horatio,
Miss Crawford as the queen, and Mr. Lacey as Francisco,
Marcellus, and Guildenstern. A local reviewer who spoke
favorably about the performance and production in general
said, however, "I will say nothing about the Ghost [portrayed
by Mr. Fredericks] as I am especially prevented to do so on

pain of severe cowhiding." (We are left several succeeding
and certainly intriguing references of this kind to Mr. Fredericks and some otherwise not recorded human interest
event.) The audience, the reviewer continued, was

> . . . large, intelligent and respectful. The
> splendid tragedy of HAMLET, with one or
> two exceptions [the Ghost?] was exceedingly
> well played. The Hamlet of Miss Barnes,
> like everything she undertakes was a delightful
> personation and nothing was wanting but a more
> masculine voice to render her performance as
> complete. Her dress, the admirable style in
> which she read the part, and her precisely
> correct conception of the character were all that
> could be desired, and the continued plaudits of
> the auditory bore ample proof to her ears that
> her efforts were properly appreciated and
> admired. [65]

During that evening Miss Barnes delivered a farewell
address in rhyming verse, which had been written for her by
"a gentleman of this city" and apparently was presented by
her in a "fervent and pleasing manner and was received by
the large audience with decided marks of approbation manifested by loud and long continued applause."[66] On such a
note, the "people's favorite" concluded her engagements in
Newark. Although she was to return several times, her
future allegiances were with Mr. E. S. Conner, whom she
married in December.

The Court Continues Briefly

The Concert Hall company continued for little more
than a week, concluding, perhaps significantly, with a benefit
for the lessee and benefactor of the season, Mr. F. P.
Medina. Mr. A. A. Addams re-appeared with the company
for this period, opening on Saturday, August 14, in Shake-

speare's Richard III. He played the Duke of Gloucester;
Mr. Fredericks, King Henry, and Miss Newkirk, Queen
Elizabeth. The evening ended with the farce, The Dumbell,
with Miss Crawford playing Eliza. On Monday for the benefit of Miss Anna Malvina, the dancer of the company, the
performance was Fazio or The Italian Wife, with Mr. Fredericks as Fazio and Miss Crawford As Bianca. This concluded with the ballet of Sylphide or The Dewdrop in which
Viola was danced by Miss Anna Malvina. Apparently nothing
was presented on Tuesday, August 17. On that day, however,
there was an announcement for a performance "tomorrow"
(Wednesday, the 18th), with Mr. Addams as Virginius in the
play of that name, Mr. Fredericks appearing as Visidius,
and Miss Malvina to repeat her Sylphide. Apparently, again,
nothing was presented Thursday, but on Friday Mr. Addams
in his third appearance with the company appeared in the
title role of Shakespeare's King Lear. Mr. Fredericks was as
the Earl of Kent and Mr. Strong was as Edward. On Saturday,
Mr. Fredericks appeared in what was to be Newark's fourth
performance of Damon and Pythias, this time with Mr. Addams as Damon and Mr. J. L. Strong as Pythias. Mr.
Addams announced his benefit and last appearance for Monday, the 23rd, at which time Shakespeare's Macbeth was
presented. Mr. Addams had the title role. Other portray-
als were: Macduff by Mr. J. B. Strong, Banquo by Mr.
Conner, King Duncan by Mr. Cooper, Prince Malcolm by
Miss Carpenter, Hecate by Mr. H. B. Hunt, Lady Macbeth
by Miss Crawford. Macbeth was followed by the farce The
Dead Shot. Within two days, another performance of Macbeth was announced, this time Miss Barnes heading the cast

in big black bold type as Lady Macbeth, Mr. Addams repeating his performance as Macbeth in the benefit for Mr. F. P.
Medina, "the worthy lessee of the establishment."[67]

Following Mr. Medina's benefit, this last somewhat
sporadic effort at establishing a legitimate stock company in
Newark was, in effect, over for the year. Despite a few
scattered productions the next few months (in which Miss
Crawford, Messrs. Addams, A. Smith, Connor, Cooper,
J. B. Strong, Byrne, and H. B. Hunt reappeared, and Newark saw Miss Ada Parker for the first time), for all prac-
tical purposes, the explosion of professional legitimate
theater in Newark in April of 1847 had concluded for that
year on August 25.

Was there not a discriminating theater audience in
Newark large enough to support a stock company which presented a "quality" fare? Were the lighter productions not
really what the audience wanted? It was, perhaps, unfair
to judge by Nickinson's ill-fated season which had the dis-
advantage of the heat of summer (hardly a season to be in-
doors anyway). Such may have been the reasoning of Mr.
James Stark who announced his return and the opening of the
theater in Newark on December 20 by informing the inhabitants that he "has become lessee of the above establishment
for a short season and that it is now being refitted and
decorated and will open with an efficient company of ladies
and gentlemen from the Park Theatre, New York, aided by
others of acknowledged talent, among which the highly celebrated Heron Family have been engaged and will appear on
Wednesday evening, the 22nd."[68] The season from December
22 to 29 (with a matinee in addition on the 25th), is exem-

plified by such productions as Old and Young or The Four
Monkeys, The Idiot Witness or The Solitary of the Piece,
Irish Tutor or New Lights, Born to Good Luck, or An Irishman's Good Fortune, as well as three acknowledgements of
the classic theater: the fifth act of Richard III, the third act
of Julius Ceasar, and "Cato's soliloquy in character."[69] Despite these last tokens, this season marked a departure from
the English or intellectual tradition and a return to the production policy that Mr. Nickinson had undertaken earlier,
with an emphasis upon popular drama, particularly the Irish
character farces, but no one cared sufficiently (certainly not
the Irish working class) for the season to be extended.

Golden Days Again

The great beginnings in 1847 were to end in December
of that year, on not too high a note. Concert Hall did not
house the legitimate theater again until the last week in April
of the following year, at which time Miss Charlotte Barnes,
then Mrs. E. S. Conner, and her husband returned to Newark at the invitation of Mr. F. P. Medina. Mr. Medina
gathered together several other performers who, along with
the "people's favorite," had been with Concert Hall from its
first days the year before and had also become favorites,
notably Messrs. H. P. Grattan, A. A. Addams, and F. S.
Chanfrau.

Under Mr. Medina's support theater blossomed again
at Concert Hall. The season continued until May 26, during
which time Newark saw the Conners in The Lady of Lyons;
Youthful Queen; Fazio, or The Italian Wife; and Mrs. Conner's own play The Forest Princess, or Two Centuries Ago,

which had been premiered in Albany the year before[70] and
was part of her newly published collection of writings. Mr.
E. S. Conner also appeared in Richelieu, the title role of
which he was to play many times and develop a reputation
for during the course of his long career.

In general the season comprised the favorite plays of
the favorite players. Indeed, the list reads as though the
queen and her royal court had never left.[71] There is one
exception, however, which should be noted. Mr. Chanfrau,
who had moved with ease the year before from Mr.
Nickinson's "popular" season to the Barnes-Fredericks'
"elite" season, had in the meantime achieved that personal
success for which all actors long. His characterization of
Mose had captured the New York public fancy. Mose was
to have many plays written for his exploits. Newark saw
the current vehicle: A Glance at New York in 1848.[72]

Aristocratic Pleasure and Democratic Work

Mr. Medina expressed quite clearly his idea of a
theater in his intention "to supply a place of amusement
where all may witness the Masterpieces of the Drama . . . ."[73]
This idea, indeed, might have been expressed by Messrs.
Sullivan and Miller when they introduced the first stock company at Concert Hall. From the beginning Concert Hall was
considered a place for all the citizens of Newark, and as
such, it exemplified a kind of democratic ideal. By infer-
ence, this democratic ideal presented opportunity for better-
ment which would create, ultimately, a nation, not of common men, but of aristocrats. Thus, in keeping with the
ideal, Mr. Medina and others could assume a theater of

masterworks, performed by master artists, for and supported by all.

The "all" of Newark consisted of approximately
30,000 in 1848. [74] Newark was a flourishing and growing
industrial center and port of entry. The building of the
Morris Canal (leading to the Pennsylvania coal fields) and
the New Jersey Railroad (now the Pennsylvania) drew a large
number of foreign-born laborers initially. As the state's
leading port, Newark continued to require more and more
workers. [75] The working classes, however, were not those
who sought the theater as a "pleasant retreat," as had our
eighteenth-century Tristram. They rather resembled those
other forebears who sought "New Work." For most of them,
home, not theater (certainly not a theater of masterpieces)
was the end of the day's duty. The "ideal," therefore,
could never become "real."

The first days and months of Concert Hall, nonetheless, were golden, and those civic-minded Newarkers who
enjoyed the theater supported the productions there. Their
support, however, was insufficient to justify a permanent
stock company playing continuously in repertory. Other at-
tempts would, of course, be made, but Concert Hall remained primarily the home of many exciting though transitory
efforts.

Notes

1. Joseph Atkinson, The History of Newark (Newark:
    William B. Guild, 1879), p. 168.

2. Ibid., p. 148; David Pierson, Narratives of Newark
    (Newark: Pierson Publishing Co., 1917), p. 228,
    234; Frank J. Urquhart, A Short History of
    Newark (Newark: Baker Printing Co., 1953),
    p. 71-77.

3.   Wilson Farrand, A Brief History of the Newark
      Academy, 1774-1792-1916, Contribution to the
      Celebration of the 250th Anniversary of the
      Founding of Newark (May, 1916), p. 5-6.

4.   See John T. Cunningham, Newark (Newark: The New
      Jersey Historical Society, 1966), p. 59.

5.   Woods's Newark Gazette (June, 1791).

6.   Ibid. (December 22, 1791).

7.   Atkinson, History of Newark, p. 199, 202.

8.   George C. D. Odell, Annals of the New York Stage, II
      (New York: Columbia University Press, 1927),
      p. 35 ff, 38, 62. See also William Dunlap,
      History of the American Theatre (New York: J. &
      J. Harper, 1832), p. 248, and Diary of William
      Dunlap (Collections of the New York Historical
      Society, 1929), I, p. 128, 131, 266, 317.

9.   Newark Gazette (October 1, 1799).

10.   Foster Rhea Dulles, America Learns to Play (New
      York: D. Appleton-Century Company, 1940), p. 84.

11.   Timothy Dwight, Travels in New England and New
      York (London, 1823), quoted in Dulles, America
      Learns to Play, p. 84.

12.   Newark Daily Advertiser (May 7-19, 1832).

13.   Ibid. (May 7, 1832); cf Odell, Annals of the New
      York Stage, III (1928), p. 577.

14.   Odell, Annals, III, p. 585.

15.   Ibid. p. 521, 530, 571, 577.

16.   See Atkinson, History of Newark, p. 193, 199ff;
      Pierson, Narratives of Newark, p. 266ff.

17.   Atkinson, Ibid. p. 189.

18.   Newark Daily Advertiser (February 2, 1847).

19.   Ibid.

20.   Atkinson, History of Newark, p. 189.

21.   Newark Daily Advertiser (February 3, 1847).

22.   Ibid., (February 16, 1847).

23. Ibid. (April 8, 1847).

24. Ibid.

25. Odell, Annals, V (1931), p. 298.

26. Newark Daily Advertiser (April 8, 1847).

27. Ibid.

28. Ibid. (April 10, 1847).

29. Ibid.

30. Ibid. (April 19-23, 1847).

31. Ibid. (April 12-17, 1847).

32. Ibid. (May 2, 1847).

33. Ibid. (May 8, 1847).

34. Oral S. Coad and Edwin Mims, Jr., "The American Stage," In Vol. 14 of The Pageant of America (New Haven: Yale University Press, 1929), p. 73.

35. Joseph N. Ireland, Records of the New York Stage from 1750-1860 (New York: T. H. Morrell, 1867), II, p. 79.

36. Arthur Hobson Quinn, A History of the American Drama from the Beginning to the Civil War (New York: F. S. Crofts, 1943), p. 260-261, 425 ff.

37. See Appendix A for recorded performances of The Captive at least three years prior to the date given by Quinn, A History of the American Drama . . ., p. 435, for the first performance.

38. Newark Daily Advertiser (May 6-17, 1847).

39. Odell, Annals, V. p. 262.

40. Newark Daily Advertiser (May 18, 1847).

41. Lloyd Morris, Curtain Time (New York: Random House Inc., 1953), p. 129.

42. Newark Daily Advertiser (May 20, 1847).

43. Ibid. (May 18-June 1, 1847). See also Odell, Annals, V, p. 262.

44. Newark Daily Advertiser (June 3-7, 1847).

45.   Coad and Mims, "American Stage," p. 174.

46.   Newark Daily Advertiser, (June 3- 7, 1847).

47.   The Temperance Advocate (May 17, 1847).

48.   Newark Daily Advertiser, The Temperance Advocate
       (June 10, 1847).

49.   The Temperance Advocate (June 10, 1847).

50.   Ibid.

51.   Bernheim, The Business of the Theatre, p. 9.

52.   Ibid., p. 20.

53.   Ibid., p. 9.

54.   Newark Daily Advertiser (June 10, 1847).

55.   Coad and Mims, "American Stage," p. 100.

56.   Odell, Annals, V, p. 289.

57.   Lloyd Morris, Curtain Time p. 130, 131.

58.   Newark Daily Advertiser (June 17- July 12, 1847).

59.   Ibid. (June 29, 1847).

60.   Ibid. (July 13, 1847).

61.   Ibid. (July 24, 1847).

62.   Ibid. (July 28- 29, 1847).

63.   Ibid. (August 4- 7, 1847).

64.   Ibid. (August 9, 1847).

65.   Temperance Advocate (August 18, 1847).

66.   Ibid.

67.   Newark Daily Advertiser (August 13- 25, 1847).

68.   Ibid. (December 20- 29, 1847).

69.   Ibid.

70.   The Temperance Advocate (July 14, 1847).

71.   Newark Daily Advertiser (April 27- May 26, 1848).

72.   "For one whole week did [Chanfrau] play this popular
       role in two New York theatres and in Newark.   He
       used to drive the nine miles with a horse and
       buggy, and reach Newark in time to close the
       performance."   T. A.   Brown, A History of the
       New York Stage (New York: Dodd, Mead, 1903),
       I, p. 302.

73.   Newark Daily Advertiser (April 26, 1848).

74.   Pierson's Newark City Directory 1858-1859 (Newark:
       B. F. Pierson, 1859).

75.   See Atkinson, History of Newark, p. 193 ff;
       Pierson, Narratives of Newark, p. 266 ff.

Chapter III

Of Diversity and Competition

From the opening of Concert Hall in 1847 to the reign
of the movie palaces in the third decade of the twentieth
century, Newark saw most of the great artists of the theater.
For more than three decades these artists appeared, with
brief exceptions, on the boards of Concert Hall--the Newark
Theatre. Whereas Philadelphia was supporting two and generally three theaters in 1850 and New York (certainly by 1850
the center of theater activity) was adding a ninth,[1] Newark
had achieved a single theater (only three years old) for a
population which had reached 38,894 and was steadily growing.[2]

It became apparent that the Theater in Newark had to
compete with the various specializations and standards represented by the nine New York theaters. The New York theaters in turn were in competition among themselves. "The
growth of the American theater," Coad and Mims inform us,
"may be said to have culminated during the fifties in a rivalry more extensive and more keen than our stage had yet
known . . . . In particular Burton, Wallack [the elder] and
Laura Keene each assembled a brilliant company and vied in
an effort to capture the most influential following."[3] This
rivalry among company managers spilled over into Newark.
Stock companies were formed to inhabit the Theater in Newark, sometimes by those experienced as managers, or by
stars who wanted to settle down into their own theater and

56

still be close to the New York center. And for a brief
period, it even looked as though there might be rivalry in
Newark.

The story of the Theater in Newark continued to be
the record of the various efforts (some long, some short) to
establish a permanent stock company at Concert Hall. As a
result, Newark not only experienced that diversity represented
in New York, but often had the additional advantage of having
what was otherwise not available in that city. All in all,
there could be distinct theater advantages for the citizens of
Newark from 1847 on. There could be and were poor periods,
of course, but that had always been true of theater--and even
New York itself was not immune.

New Theaters for Old?

Even theater buildings feel upon bad days. Sometimes
they fell as their section of a city declined in fashion. Often
they were blamed for creating the disreputable. As late as
1845 The [New York] Broadway Journal protested "the effect
theatres invariably have in the neighborhood where they have
been built [by attracting] dram shops, billiard rooms, and
other equivocal resorts for the profligate and idle."[4]
Concert Hall, built as it was above the Volunteer Fire
Department and stables, might have housed a kind of "re-
sort," yet the neighborhood could hardly be called disreputable as directly across the street from Concert Hall
stood Library Hall.

Something, however, happened to the reputation of the
"place," Concert Hall, in less than two years after its opening. The Advertiser, of September 23, 1848, praised the

Moravian Singers who had appeared at Concert Hall the night
before, but deplored the meagreness of the audience. "But
we would be charitable," the writer continued, "and hope
that the disinclination was for the place and not the entertainment . . . . This will be ascertained this evening when the
singers repeat their concert in the new Library Hall." Unfortunately history did not record what was ascertained.

Legitimate theater found its way back to the stage of
Concert Hall, however, late in 1849. Despite this, concern
was evidenced that "in a city boasting the popualtion that
Newark does, there is no appropriate building dedicated to
the Drama."[5] As a result, the Mercury reported on December 28, 1849, the understanding "that [there] is in contempla-
tion to erect in this city an elegant structure for the exhibi-
tion of Dramatic entertainments . . . ." Hope was expressed in December that the following summer would find
in Newark a theater erected which would be worthy of the
city. "Those who remember the pleasure afforded by the
representations of Wallack and Miss Barnes, must be anxious
for an opportunity again, under more favorable circumstances,
of witnessing like efforts of histrionic talent."[6]

Concert Hall fell upon bad days early in its career.
The neighborhood was not at fault, apparently, nor was it
the result of puritanical prejudice against theater. Rather,
public opinion against Concert Hall was a reaction against the
owner and management of the building (which will generally
be the case through this narrative). An article in the
Mercury (October 5, 1849) informed its readers that the company presently performing was "crippled by want of machinery
[and scenery] too shabby for such audiences as in the past

have graced the Hall." It was a mistake, the writer also
noted, "to imagine that anything [Italics mine] will do for
this city, for its proximity to New York has rendered us
familiar with the best actors, and we are apt to demand too
much rather than too little . . . ."

Improvements were made for the staging of plays,
some repainting was done, and Newark continued (though somewhat unevenly) to have some bright theater days at Concert
Hall. No new theaters were to be erected, but an existing
hall, Military Hall, housed legitimate theater companies
briefly in 1852 and 1853. Thus competition, in the form of
a second theater in Newark, loomed for Concert Hall. This
undoubtedly had much to do with the decision in 1853 to make
extensive alterations and improvements in Newark's first
theater.

Military Hall As The Theater, 1852

The life of Military Hall as Newark's legitimate
theater was brief but important. The neglect of Concert Hall
had increasingly made it unattractive to audience and performers alike. Military Hall permitted Newark the continuing opportunity to witness legitimate theater and so doing gave im-
petus to the remodeling and improvement of Concert Hall.

The first company which appeared at Military Hall was
the Bowery Company in August, 1852. New York's Bowery
Theatre company had been displaced from its stage in late
July by a successful rivalry between two magicians which
lasted until August 21. [7] The "homeless" company, under
the management of Henry Seymour, played in Newark from
August 2 to August 21--at which time they could return home.

They were followed within a few weeks by a new dramatic
company, which opened at Military Hall, "one of the most
beautiful and spacious in our state."[8]

On September 23rd the new Dramatic Company, comprising "several old favorites of the city and others well-
known on the New York stage," opened at Military Hall.   Mr.
William Henderson, the acting and stage manager of the new
company, announced that "it will be conducted in all its
various departments with a strict regard for producing each
piece with correct costumes and a talented company, [and]
that no vulgarity will be permitted on the stage."[9]   Newark
responded to the new company at the new theater.   The reader may like to select the "old favorites" from among the
opening company: Messrs. William M. Fleming, Wise, Mac-
Donald, Denis, Henderson, A. H. Davenport, Weaver,
Thorpe, and Pemberton, and the Misses Mitchell and Wyette
and Mrs. Thorpe.

The Henderson company continued to bring back some
of the "old favorites."   Each visiting star brought variety to
the theater as he performed the plays and roles with which
he had come to be associated.   On September 29, 1852, Mr.
T. D. Rice joined the company in several of his characters,
and on October 12, Mr. and Mrs. Barney Williams added
their Irish characterizations.   November brought back Mr.
F. S. Chanfrau and introduced Newark to the "notorious"
Lola Montez in The Maid of Saragossa the next day.   December saw Mr. and Mrs. Rea, Miss Malvina, and Mrs.
Morton (of Niblo's Garden), a long-run hit-- The Newark
Firemen, and the end of the Henderson season.

At Concert Hall: The Newark Firemen

       Not all of this exciting season was presented at Military Hall. As of November 1, the Henderson company moved its operations to the elegantly refitted (including new stage decorations) Concert Hall, which resumed, as Lyceum, its role as the home of legitimate theater in Newark. Appropriately, The Newark Firemen opened there on December 4, 1852. Newark's own local drama of its firemen (including scenes of the city), ran for eleven consecutive performances.[10] How much of this success was the result of the Fire Company being housed on either side of the Market Street entrance is purely a matter of conjecture. It is interesting to note, however, that the first event to take place on the stage of Newark's first theater had been for the benefit of the volunteer firemen. Almost six years later the first long-run production was a play about Newark firemen.

Military Hall Returns, 1853

       During the first three quarters of 1853 plans were being made and put into action for the remodeling of Concert Hall. As a result, Military Hall again entered the history of Newark's legitimate theater. On July 2, under the management of Messrs. Griffiths and Mathews, "a number of actors of both sexes who have already become favorites here," opened in the perennially favorite, Lady of Lyons. Along with a "new stage, new scenery, and new dresses," the new Dramatic Company consisted of the following: Miss Mitchell, Miss Stephens, from Wallack's; Mrs. Griffiths, Mrs. Monell from St. Charles Theatre; Mrs. Emma Mitchell, Miss Mar-

shals, Mr. Davenport from the Broadway; Mr. Glenn from
the Bowery; Mr. Pilgrim, the popular author and actor;
Mr. Everett from the Charleston Theatre; Mr. Floyd from
the St. Charles; Mr. Durant from Wallack's; Mr. Baldwin
from the National Theatre, Boston. [11]

The Company at Military Hall, (an establishment
announced as being well ventilated) opened "under favorable
auspices and liberal patronage." The company continued
"before a large and respectable audience." This patronage
was apparently so liberal that, aside from placing their initial advertisement in the newspaper, the Military Hall Company relied upon word of mouth and an occasional cultural
item in the Advertiser for the continuance of its season.
"A crowded house on Saturday Evening [July 23] testified to
their success in pleasing the public," so the management
added to the company Mr. Allen; Mrs. Carman and her
daughter Laura, a danseuse; Mr. and Miss McCarthy,
vocalists, "and others." The Griffiths-Mathews season
closed, nonetheless, on July 30. [12]

In less than two weeks, Military Hall presented a
short season under the management of Mr. Robert Marsh.
From August 15 to September 1 the Marsh Company presented Uncle Tom's Cabin. One year before (in New York,
August 1852), the first dramatization of Mrs. Stowe's novel
had been presented unsuccessfully at Purdy's National Theatre. Currently, at the same theater, a new version for the
G. C. Howards had been creating a sensation for almost a
month. Mr. Marsh, undoubtedly capitalizing on the New
York publicity, presented the play with the "infant wonder"
little Mary Guerneau Marsh as Eva, supported by Mrs.

Williams as Cassy, Miss C. Taylor as Topsy, Miss Johnson
as Aunt Ophelia, Mr. Turner as Legree, [although on August
22nd he is listed for the role of George Harris, the character of Legree being absent from the cast listing], Mr.
Spencer as St. Clare, Mr. LeMoyne as Deacon Perry,
Mr. Marsh, himself, as Uncle Tom, Mr. Lennox as Phineas
Fletcher, and Mr. Bradshaw as Marks. Uncle Tom's Cabin
enjoyed an "overcrowded house" and "increased popularity."[13]

     With the closing of Uncle Tom's Cabin, Military Hall
removed itself from the history of the legitimate theater in
Newark.   Until the reopening of Concert Hall as "the New
Theatre" in October, 1853, with the brief season of Mr.
Strong's Company, Newark was to be amused by the ori-
ginal troupe of Chinese jugglers and the Fakir of Sheba, the
German Newarkers' Saengerbund, and a lecture on "Women's
Rights."   But let us first go back a few years.

Players and Companies at Concert Hall

     Despite mismanagement of funds, and backstage
quarrels, inclement weather, and a lethargic public, worn-
out facilities and potential competition, Concert Hall and the
legitimate theater in Newark persisted.   Actors continued to
play Newark, often with the hope of establishing a permanent
company.   Some of their engagements were long, but none
had the "permanence" of several years of a continuing company or single management.   Some, however, came close,
while others made several efforts.

Stars Against Odds, 1849

     In 1849, several luminaries appeared on the boards of

Concert Hall. Although acclaimed, the shabbiness of the
house mitigated against their success. From October 3 to
November 3, 1849, the Mercury recorded the nightly performances of Mr. Barney Williams, Mr. and Mrs. E. S.
Conner, Mr. T. D. Rice, and Mr. F. S. Chanfrau. After
a brief respite, the Mercury announced on November 19 that
Mr. Chapman (manager) planned to keep Concert Hall open
through the winter.

        Of this continuing effort, the periodicals of the day
provide only intermittent records. Performances were given
on December 8 and were still being given on April 5, June 8,
and July 15, 1850. This last date marked a complimentary
benefit to Mr. Chapman, who apparently had suffered financial reverses during the summer. During this period Newark's own citizen, Mr. A. J. Frost, appeared on the boards
with Mrs. G. Chapman, Mrs. Hautonville, Mr. Redmond
Ryan, Mr. J. R. Scott, and Mr. and Mrs. Howard.

                        Chanfrau's Newark
        The name of F. S. Chanfrau was well-known to the
Newark theater-goer, both before and after his great success
as Mose, the fire b'hoy. This phenomenal personal triumph
had led the doubtless energetic Mr. Chanfrau for a period
of time to play successively at two theaters in New York
and at Concert Hall in Newark. He had undertaken the
management of the New York Chatham in 1848, reopening it
as Chanfrau's New National. He retired from its management on April 12, 1850. [14] Shortly after this Mr. Chanfrau
reappeared in Newark and announced the opening of the Newark Theatre for the winter season.

Whether or not Mr. Chanfrau had intended to establish a company at Concert Hall is not known. He may have
turned to Newark as a pleasant respite from the demands of
popularity in New York, which had kept him appearing in one
new Mose adventure after another. Lloyd Morris tells us
that "the role brought him fame and wealth, but he detested
it as an inescapable, tedious burden that had thwarted his
aspirations."[15] Whereas the New York audience was indif-
ferent to his serious roles, the Newark audience (which had
known him before in serious roles) asked: "Cannot Mr. Chanfrau give us Don Caezar [sic] de Bazan during his stay?"[16]

Mr. Chanfrau opened his winter season in Newark,
on October 5, 1850, with Don Caesar de Bazan. On Monday, October 7, he undertook the role of Claude Melnotte in
The Lady of Lyons "supported by a talented and powerful company," according to the Advertiser the next day. Unfortunately there is a lapse in recorded evidence until we get to
October 26. That Mr. Chanfrau's season had continued is
suggested by the announcement on that date of a benefit for
John Weaver. Mr. N. B. Clark and Miss Annie Sinclair
presented "by request . . . the moral, domestic Temperance drama" entitled The Drunkard.

Later events suggest that Mr. Chanfrau's winter
season was merely a curtain raiser. One may wonder
whether or not he included one of the Mose plays in the
season. One can imagine him relaxing with the Newark fire
b'hoys in the station below the theater, giving them Mose,
then enacting one of the serious roles he liked that night
on the stage of Concert Hall.

Players and Plays, 1851

The winter season, which Mr. Chanfrau had ushered
in, culminated (on January 18, 1851) in a six-week season
under Messrs. Lovell and King. Other than for a two-day
return engagement of Mr. Chanfrau at the end of May, a
brief engagement of Miss Laura Addison, the English actress,
in December, and two performances of the German Theatre,[17]
the Lovell-King season marked the last of significant recorded legitimate theater at Concert Hall until it was remodeled
and reopened in 1853.

From January 18 to March 1, Lovell and King's
Lyceum presented a full and varied program of productions
with a company comprising not only the lessees, Lovell and
King, and the Stage manager Mr. Clarke, but also Mrs.
Lovell, Mr. Joe Cowell, Mr. F. C. Wemyss (the Francis
Courtney Wemyss?), Mr. J. Proctor, and a Miss Jefferson,
among others. For their opening production they presented
Lady of Lyons with Mr. and Mrs. Lovell in the parts of
Claude Melnotte and Pauline. They next presented "for the
first time the grand Oriental spectacle" Bluebeard, with new
scenery by Mr. Culvert and machinery by Mr. D. Briggs.
The cast for this production included N. B. Clarke as Abo-
milque; Mr. King as Selim; Mr. Cowell as Sacabac; and
Miss Ruhamah as Irena. A local reviewer spoke of Blue-
Beard as "a great entertainment [and] triumphant success, . . .
with all its beautiful scenery, machinery. It was received
with shouts of applause by a delighted audience. The great
comedian, Mr. Joe Cowell [played] three characters."[18]

During his engagement with the Lyceum, Mr. Cowell

was also seen in Turnpike Gate, the title role in Poor Pillicody, in Tom Cringle, The Fire Raisers (in which he undertook two characters), Turning the Tables, The Stranger,
Sketches in India, Rent Day (a domestic drama), and as
Polonius in Hamlet.   His re-engagements with the company
permitted him to add such plays as Mazeppa, and Rockwood
or Dick Turpin The Highwayman, both roles which the ladies
would soon take over.   On January 27, the American tragedian, Mr. E. Eddy (whom we shall meet again), joined the
Lyceum company for an engagement of six nights.   During
this time, the Newark company essayed, with Mr. Eddy
figuring prominently, La Tour de Nesle, Othello, (Mr. Eddy
in the title role), The Stranger, Rent Day, Richard III, and
Hamlet. [19]

   All in all, Lovell and King's Lyceum presented Newark, in the little more than six weeks of its existence, with
quite a varied program of productions.   There was something
for everyone.   From the Oriental spectacle dramas such as
Bluebeard to the new Equestrian novelties such as Putnam or
The Iron Son of 76 and Mazeppa or The Wild Horse of
Tartary; from the ever-popular Lady of Lyons to such Irish
dramas as Rebel or The Death Fetch of the Doomed; from
the burletta, Mummy, to the tragedies of Shakespeare, the
lessees made a strong bid for the establishment of a permanent theater company in Newark.   However, despite Captain
Hand of the Washington Continentals (a military company) at-
tending the theater and "adding much to the large audience,"
and the appearance of "Jim Crow" Rice, who appeared for the
benefit of Mr. C. A. King, [20] Newark's Lyceum closed its
doors March 1, 1851.

Concert Hall Remodeled, 1853

     A request was made in the Advertiser on May 3, 1853,
by Messrs. Edward E. Jones and Richmond Ward for "plans
and drawings from architects or from those who are acquaint-
ed with the wants of a room for the . . . purposes" of a
musical hall, Concert Hall "being now ready for alteration."
On August 3 an article informed the Advertiser readers that
extensive improvements were being made and that "when
completed [Concert Hall] will be the largest and finest room
in the city for musical and histrionic performances. The
entire building is occupied for one purpose, the floors having
been lowered from the third to the first story . . . ." The
stables which had comprised the ground floor of the original
structure and had undoubtedly greatly contributed to the audiences' discomfiture as well as the building's physical decay,
were now removed. The article went on to state:

> The length including the stage, is 110 feet,
> the width 50, the height 33. The capacity
> will be sufficient to accomodate with seats
> 1000 persons, and arrangements can be
> made for 1400. The audience room 70 by
> 50 feet, comprising a parquette of nearly
> the entire depth and a gallery extending all
> around, is all included in one apartment,
> and it is intended to have no distinction of
> prices, thus preventing rowdyism and the
> introduction of improper characters. It will
> be finished with circular and convenient seats,
> heated by furnace, well ventilated and firmly
> secured by brick foundations supporting the
> beams and pillars. The stage is 40 feet deep
> with a proscenium 26 feet high and 33 wide,
> 2 private boxes on each side, a gallery at the
> back of the scene shifters, a dressing room
> behind it 50 by 15 feet, and apartments beneath
> for the orchestra, and such ghosts and other

> subterranean personages as Hamlet or King
> Richard may be under the necessity of seeing.
> Arrangements may be made to enclose a large
> portion of the stage in parlor scenery for concerts.
> The entrance on Market St. will be 11 feet wide,
> with a ceiling of 12 feet, and two stories high,
> a fine arched window being inserted in the upper
> story. The whole, it is expected, will be com-
> pleted in about six weeks, and will supply a
> deficiency long felt in our city, and which has
> prevented us from seeing and hearing many of
> the wonders that astonish our neighbors in New
> York. The proprietors are determined that the
> exhibitions shall be consonant with the character
> of the Hall, and to guarantee to the public such
> amusements as shall be acceptable to all our
> citizens. [21]

Apparently dropping floors and adding seats, among
the various alterations noted, took longer to effect than the
originally estimated six weeks. It was more like twelve
weeks when the new Concert Hall was reopened. On October
13, 1853, Newark's Theater was to be "christened" by a
musical event just as it had been originally, in 1847. Madame
Sontag, whose appearance was to "mark an event to the progress of Concerts in this city," opened at the "beautiful hall"
which was "an ornament to the city, displaying the enterprise
and taste of its proprietors, and is such a one as has long
been needed in Newark." [22] If Madame Sontag's performance
was not up to her heralded best, she was nonetheless greeted
by a "beaming" audience whose "animated countenances" comprised "such an array of beauty, fashion, and sterling worth,
as we only see on some remarkable occasion." The only flaw
to this outstanding event in such a "handsomely lighted saloon"
was a "frigid atmosphere, especially in the lower part of
the house." This made it rather uncomfortable for some

members of the audience and very likely had its effect upon
Madame Sontag.[23] Despite a heating problem, Newark's
"new theater" had an auspicious reopening and in less than
two weeks a theater company under the management of
J. B. Strong announced a season of plays. Once again,
Concert Hall was the proud and appropriate home of legitimate theater in Newark.

At the New Concert Hall (Newark Theatre)

Following the gala reopening of Concert Hall in 1853
with Madame Sontag, Mr. J. B. Strong opened the legitimate
theater season with Knowles' The Hunchback. His company
epitomized the self-contained stock company playing in repertory. As such it emulated the trend exemplified in New York
by J. W. Wallack and others. This trend differed from the
old stock and star system (with which Concert Hall opened
in 1847) primarily in its independence from the guest star
and its resultant greater emphasis upon the ensemble. (Nonetheless, even this concept accepted the stars and often produced them.) Mr. and Mrs. J. B. Strong were the leading
players in their company. They essayed the roles of Claude
Melnotte and Pauline in a performance of Bulwer's [sic] play
which, for some reason, they titled The Lady of Dumas.
Their season closely resembled that of Wallack's in New
York, particularly with its emphasis upon the English plays.[25]

Scattered seasons continued to typify the new Newark
Theatre. Names now familiar continued to reappear, along
with new ones. Pages of the daily newspaper continued to
announce periodically a new effort at the Theatre. Then
there would be no more announcements. In general, the

Newark Theatre continued to need periodic improving and
eventually got it.   Out of the repetition of efforts, similarity
of engagements, and dearth of recorded evidence, however,
there are two items which should be noted.

The first is primarily of local significance: the apparent dedication of the theater in Newark of Mrs. Amelia
Parker and Mr. Tom Wemyss.   Both had extended associa-
tions with the Theatre as lessees, managers, and players.
The second item is not unique to Newark.   Rather, its significance (many times discussed) relates to a complex which
is national.   The second item is Uncle Tom's Cabin.

Came to Laugh, Remained to Pray

Uncle Tom's Cabin reappeared many times in Newark
from its first production in 1853 to the end of our narrative.
Although the first dramatization of Mrs. Stowe's novel was
unsuccessful, the version by George L. Aiken which Mr.
George C. Howard had commissioned for himself, his wife,
and their daughter Cordelia, became a phenomenal success.
In New York the Howard production was performed over two
hundred successive times.   It brought a new audience to the
theater.   For some it was not unlike going to church.   Even
the most sophisticated came under its spell.   For the American theater it presaged the revolutionary change from repertory to long-run which contributed to the death of the stock
system, and evidenced the growing interest of the audience
in plays which were topical or timely. [25]

The Howard production of Uncle Tom's Cabin came to
Newark several times and always played to full houses.   It
was not untypical for several hundred people to fail to gain

admission.[26] In 1859 the Howards apparently had several
engagements in Newark and included other works in their
repertoire.   An extant program for the Newark Theatre
(February 16, 1859)[27] announced the Howards in Tom Tit
which C. W. Taylor (author of the first, unsuccessful version
of Uncle Tom's Cabin) had written expressly for them, and
Dred of the Dismal Swamp.   Later in the year, on December
9, the Advertiser announced that Mr. G. C. Howard had become manager of the Newark Theatre.   His season as manager did not have, however, anything approximating the longevity of Uncle Tom's Cabin.

As we move into the sixth decade of the nineteenth
century, it is not inappropriate that we pause in our narrative with the G. C. Howards' production of Uncle Tom's
Cabin.   Both the forthcoming war between the States and
the revolutionary changes coming in the theater had seeds
planted by Uncle Tom's Cabin.

Notes

1.   See Arthur H. Wilson, A History of the Philadelphia
       Theatre 1835-1855 (Philadelphia: University of
       Pennsylvania Press, 1935), p. 408-430; George
       C. D. Odell, Annals of the New York Stage, VI
       (New York: Columbia University Press, 1931);
       Oral S. Coad and Edwin Mims, Jr., "The American
       Stage," The Pageant of America (New Haven: Yale
       University Press, 1929), XIV, p. 74.

2.   Pierson's Newark City Directory 1858-1859 (Newark:
       B. F. Pierson, 1859).

3.   Coad and Mims, "American Stage," p. 184.

4.   Quoted in Alfred L. Bernheim, The Business of the
       Theatre (New York: Benjamin Blom, Inc., 1964),
       p. 19.

5.   Newark Daily Mercury (December 18, 1849).

6. Ibid. (April 27, 1839).

7. Odell, Annals, VI, p. 139.

8. Newark Daily Advertiser (August 4, 1852).

9. Ibid. (September 21, 1852).

10. Ibid. (October 29-December 4, 16, 1852).

11. Ibid. (July 1-2, 1853).

12. Ibid. (July 25, 30, 1853).

13. Ibid. (August 15, 16, 22, 1853).

14. Odell, Annals, V, p. 455, 548.

15. Lloyd Morris, Curtain Time (New York: Random House, Inc., 1953), p. 135.

16. Newark Daily Mercury (October 29, 1849).

17. Newark Daily Mercury (May 31, 1851); Newark Daily Advertiser (May 14, 17, December 15, 16, 1851).

18. Newark Daily Advertiser (January 18, 20, 1851).

19. Ibid. (January 20-- February 27, 1851).

20. Ibid. (February 26, 27, 1851).

21. Ibid. (August 3, 1853).

22. Ibid. (October 11-12, 1853).

23. Ibid. (October 14, 1853).

24. Newark Daily Advertiser (October 25, 27, 1853); Barnard Hewitt, Theatre U.S.A.: 1668 to 1957 (New York: McGraw-Hill, 1959), p. 181.

25. Coad and Mims, "American Stage," p. 196; Hewitt, Theatre U. S. A., p. 171-77.

26. Newark Daily Advertiser (November 25, 1859).

27. Theatre Program Files, New Jersey Historical Society, Newark.

Chapter IV

Of Revolutions and Relaxation

The growths in population and prosperity of Newark
which were noted in the fourth decade of the nineteenth century had made great strides during the fifth decade. New
buildings were constructed to meet the demands of business
and housing. Around 500 structures, including five churches,
had been erected in one year alone. There had been a
severe financial crisis in 1857, but by spring of the next
year all was well again.[1] The population at that time had
increased to more than 64,000. In fact, Newark embraced
more than half of the population of Essex County.[2] A city
the size of Newark in 1857 should have been able to support
at least one theater. But as we have seen, despite spurts
of activity, the theater had not been able to establish a permanent position in the life of the city.

Where, O Where Is Culture Found?

Scattered brief seasons of legitimate theater, odds
and ends of minstrelsy, lecturing, and concertizing could
hardly satisfy the cultural needs of a city such as Newark.
The greater percent of the populace, who had time for little
more than work, were not culture-minded. On the other
hand, there was that other (granted smaller) segment of the
public which wanted and sought theater. For both groups,
entertainment in general was readily accessible. To get it,

Newark citizens had only to travel to New York. Newark
newspapers not only carried advertisements for the New York
theaters and the various other allurements of the city, but
for over-night accomodations as well. A not untypical advertisement is the one for New York's Union Dining Saloon
"which will be found open at a late hour in the evening, thus
affording the citizens of Newark who may be detained in the
city [New York] by the public entertainments . . . an opportunity of obtaining some refreshments previous to returning
home."[3]

     Newarkers who did not get to New York found their
major source of entertainment in the minstrel. It may well
be that every minstrel company had played at least one performance in Newark. By 1860, one might assume that Newark was home base for the old companies and a training camp
for the new ones emerging. In many instances Newarkers
would find in a new minstrel company many members of
another company which had visited their city a month or so
before. In other cases, a new company would in reality be
only a new name for an old company. For example, in 1860
Wood's minstrels appeared in March, and in April Bud-
worth's (late Wood's) appeared. Then, too, parts of a company (carrying their name with them) would merge with another company, while the rest merged with still another company. The public may have found it somewhat confusing to
have, in less than a month, three minstrel troupes calling
themselves, in various combinations, Campbell's, Rumsey
and Newcomb's, Mat Pell's, and Hooley's.[4]

     Thus, as we move into the sixth decade of the nine-
teenth century, we find Newark an industrial adjunct to New

York City, which by now was firmly established as the theater center of the Nation.   For Newarkers, the Nation's center
was in their own front yard.   Those who required it could
easily find both relaxation and culture.   Light fare, such as
the minstrels provided, was otherwise sufficient for the
periodic needs of the general Newark public.   A light, less
intellectual fare continued to satisfy the needs of the general
public, but the nature of this fare changed in the first years
of the 1860's and the "Free and Easy"[5] took the place of the
old minstrel.

Changes were occurring in the legitimate theater itself.
The stirrings of a new realism--whether it be eloquent (as
with Edwin Booth) or emotional (as with Matilda Heron)[6]--
were growing in pressure.   The Civil War, although tempo-
rarily disrupting the prosperity of the theater, revived, on
the other hand, romantic adventure extravaganzas, along with
patriotic, national, and local-color plays.   During the war,
as is apparently always the case, theatrical activity boomed.[7]
In Newark, the wave of such prosperity at the close of the
war again lifted many hopes for the establishment of a permanent stock company.

Calm Before The Storm

The theater in New York might be enjoying generally
prosperous times, but the theater in Newark seemed to be
enjoying only the sporadic encampment of a traveling star or
brief season of a company.   One week, in May, 1860, brought
Miss Maggie Mitchell, Mr. A. H. Davenport, and Mr. T. A.
T. Neafie to the banks of the Passaic.   Newark theater-goers
met Mr. Davenport some years earlier, but were meeting

Miss Mitchell and Mr. Neafie for the first time.   Although
Mr. Neafie was to reappear many times at the Newark
Theatre, this brief engagement was Newark's only encounter
with the "fascinating" Miss Mitchell.   Newark saw her in
The Four Sisters.   Two years later in New York she created
her most popular character, Fanchon, the Cricket.   It was
this character, Odell tells us, "which was thereafter most
closely identified with her fame."[8]   This tiny comedienne
(along with Charlotte Crabtree later) was particularly successful in impersonations of the young.

        The Newark Theatre had no further encounters with
legitimate theater until October.   At that time a touring company of American Indians presented three performances of,
interestingly enough, Pochohantos.   But, of course, the real
events of 1860 were those of the conflict between the States.
South Carolina seceded from the Union.   Most events in
October and early November gave way to politics and elec-
tioneering.   Following the election of Abraham Lincoln as
16th President of the United States the cultural life of Newark resumed with a brief appearance of Wood's Minstrels
and a matinee and evening performance of The Drunkard or
The Fallen Saved.   In December Mr. William Burke and
company presented a holiday season which opened with the
classic tale of friendship, Damon and Pythias.

A Flurry of Activity
        After the initial shock of civil war there were efforts
which recognized a new need for entertainment.   Lieut. E.
F. Marden leased the Newark Theatre and announced a
season beginning with Harrold Hawk on August 31, 1861.

Lieut. Marden had the honor to present for the first time
in Newark Boucicault's Colleen Bawn, which had met with
popular acclaim at Laura Keane's Theatre in New York the
year before.   It met with success in Newark and was given
an additional performance.   On September 9, Mr. T. A. T.
Neafie joined the company in the title role of Hamlet for
which he "drew an overwhelming house . . . ."   His benefit
and last appearance in Richard III on September 12 seemed
also to mark the end of Lieut. Marden's season.[9]   Things
were looking up, however, for the end of October introduced
a flurry of theater activities which continued through the end
of the year.

On October 28 the popular New York actor Edward
Eddy (whom Newarkers had seen before, in 1851) opened at
the Newark Theatre in Virginius and Artful Dodger.   Mr.
Eddy who had had, according to Odell "an orgy of managing
one theatre after another," had ended an engagement at the
New Bowery on October 26.   For the last few seasons his
engagements at New York's New Bowery had been a major
attraction.   In Newark he was seen in Jack Cade, Le Tour
de Nesle, Last Days of Pompeii, and Pizarro among others.
He was assisted by Mrs. W. G. Jones through November 1
at which time she left to reopen (the next day) the New
Bowery where she was one of the "main props."[10]

Plays Patriotic and Timely

Boucicault's Octoroon and Hidden Hand, each running
for a week, were to follow Mr. Eddy on the Newark boards
beginning November 4, 1861.   Boucicault's Octoroon had
opened on December 5, 1859, at the New York Winter Garden

with a cast which included the playwright, A. H. Davenport, and Joseph Jefferson. Mr. Ponisi, also a member of that first production, appeared with the Newark Company, for which he was also acting stage manager. Others in the Newark cast included Messrs. Sefton, Tilton, G. W. Thompson, Charles Foster, and the Misses Kimberly and Hyde. Miss Kimberly probably portrayed Zoe, the role which was advertised in New York a year later as having been played by her "nearly 600 times in all the principal cities of the Union."[11] Except for Mr. Foster, the same cast appeared the next week (beginning November 11) in Hidden Hand, to which was added Mr. Clarke (very likely C. W. whose name reappears a few weeks later in the theater advertisements).

Within the month Newark audiences saw a third play by the popular playwright, Dion Boucicault. The Poor of New York had dramatized the financial panic of 1857, following the event by a month. The plays of Boucicault had proved to be great successes, as E. J. West informs us, "largely on the basis of what seemed timeliness and contemporaneity of subject and theme and on the score of the necessarily increasing realism of acting methods required by contemporary costume worn in or in front of contemporary scenes."[12] The Octoroon, for example, had followed John Brown's raid on Harper's Ferry (October 18, 1859) by little more than a month and further exemplified the author's sensitivity to timeliness.

The more famous Uncle Tom's Cabin (with Fanny Beane as Eva) returned with appropriate subject timeliness along with the similarly appropriate new plays, Patriot's Dream and John Jones of the War Office. These (and The

Poor of New York) played in repertory through most of
November, 1861, to which was added November 30, The
Newark Firemen, undoubtedly with new war-time significance. [13]

The first week in December brought Newarkers that
variety of productions which comprised the repertory of Mr.
C. W. Clarke including Eustache Baudin, Charlotte Temple,
Don Caesar de Bazan, and the Perennial Lady of Lyons.
Miss Annie Frost, who had been featured earlier in Patriot's
Dream, played with Mr. Clarke in Eustache Baudin. From
then until December 26 the Newark audience saw also Mr.
Joseph Proctor, Mr. G. H. Hill, Mr. W. M. Ward and
for a brilliant conclusion, Mr. and Mrs. J. W. Wallack,
Jr., and Mr. E. L. Davenport. [14]

Mr. Joseph Proctor, a Newark returnee since 1850,
came into "the region of stars" in February, 1859, at The
Bowery, but was to take what Odell calls his "valuable as-
sets" away from the New York stage until February, 1863. [15]
The diversity of Mr. Proctor's repertory, during the nine
days he played in Newark, was attested to by such productions as Nick of the Woods, George or The Armorer of
Tyre, Outahlanchet, The Lion of the Forest, Macbeth, and
Ambition. (Altogether Mr. Proctor sounds like a fascinating
man.) Mr. W. M. Ward added among others Vasco Pares
(in 3 acts and 7 tableaux) and Show Your Colors or The
Stars and Stripes. [16] It must be remembered that this was
war-time.

On December 24 and 26, direct from their brief but
brilliant season at the New Bowery, the Wallack-Davenport
team brought their production of Damon and Pythias to the
Newark Theatre. This climax to the Newark Theatre season

coincided not inappropriately with the Christmas season--
hardly a joyous one for a nation at war against itself.
For this first wartime holiday the production of Damon and
Pythias must have had additional significance and have presented a moving plea for friendship, brotherhood, and peace
on earth.

Diversification with Cool White

The first two months of 1862 find legitimate theater
absent from Newark. On March 3, however, the Theatre
"having been newly decorated and painted . . . opened for
the season" under the management of Mr. Cool White. Mr.
White, who had begun his career as a minstrel man, brought
to Newark his production of Uncle Tom's Cabin. He appeared as Sambo the slave with Mr. Alexander as Uncle Tom
and Mrs. Thompson as Topsy. Despite bad weather, Uncle
Tom's Cabin opened to a good audience. A local observer
noted that the building "has been much improved in appearance and is now very credible."[17]

Mr. White presented Newark audiences with a light
and diversified season ranging from a patriotic piece The
Roll of the Drum through such ethnic pieces as The Irish
Emigrant to a local drama written by a gentleman of Newark, The New Jersey First or Scenes on the Potomac. A-
round the middle of the month Mr. White began diversifying
his performances with humorous Ethiopian minstrel entertainments. His burlesque, Father Kemp's Old Folks, was
considered admirable. All in all, Mr. White's endeavors
to establish a theater which he felt would be worthy of support were well supported by the press, if not sufficiently sup-

ported by the public. It should be noted, however, that
this season brought back to Newark one of the attractions of
Concert Hall's first year of operation.

Kate Denin, now Kate Denin Ryan, Sam Ryan, her
husband, together with the Ryan children appeared for "six
nights only" beginning March 24. They presented such works
as Hidden Hand, Our American Cousin, and Joseph and His
Brethren. Advertisements suggest that the Ryans may also
have appeared in the operetta Jenny Lind. It is more likely,
however, that the operetta, along with the Ethiopian entertainments, was a part of Mr. White's theatrical diversification,
utilizing the talents of the singing members of his company.[18]

For the week following the last appearance of the
Ryans (March 29) several novelties were produced at the
Theatre under Cool White's direction. Following this, Mr.
White terminated his efforts in Newark creating a decided
lack of amusement for the local audiences. Mr. White was
to return, however, within a few weeks with one of the
sensations of the day. Prior to this there was an apparently
still-born effort to reopen the theater with Louise Wells,
William Derr, and James Pilgrim in Mazeppa and "other
horse pieces."[19] Possibly this effort conflicted with new
negotiations on the part of Mr. White. At any rate, Newark
had to wait for the popular "horse pieces" until Miss Kate
Fisher's arrival. In the meantime Mr. White reopened the
theater as the Newark Lyceum the next week, April 28, and
brought Newark the realism of Camille.

Matilda Heron and Realism
The announcement (April 24) of the engagement of

Matilda Heron in her famous role as Camille apparently
created "quite a sensation among our dramatic amateurs."
For this event the theater was cleaned, painted, and decorated with a new drop curtain which was described as being
"at once rich, tasty and artistic." Miss Heron, who had
taken rooms at Lockwood's, made her first Newark appearance in the role she had been portraying for the past seven
years with unprecedented success. [20] A local reviewer noted
that she

> was greeted last evening by a large and re-
> munerative audience and the performances
> altogether were a complete success. Miss
> Heron never represented the character of
> Camille, with which she has become so
> peculiarly identified, more satisfactorily to
> herself or her audience [had he been traveling
> with her for seven years?]. She was well
> sustained by the company in all their various
> parts, especially that of Armand in which Mr.
> Loveday almost, if not quite, divided the
> honors of the evening with Miss Heron, who
> was twice complimented with calls before the
> curtain. [21]

A more personal review of Camille appeared in the
form of a letter to the editor by Mr. Anno Domini. He
wrote:

> I commenced this article with the intention of
> giving you a little screed on Camille as
> portrayed by Miss Heron and a general
> dissertation on the Newark Lyceum [however,
> intention notwithstanding] Miss Heron's rendition
> of the somewhat anomalous character of Camille
> is most touching and truthful; the stock com-
> pany is first rate and the Lyceum is tastily
> and neatly fitted up . . . . I must defer my
> criticism on the acting of Camille for this
> time, . . . my notes are so obliterated with
> tears (a man that could sit with dry eyes
> through Matilda Heron's rendition of Camille

ought to peel onions for a livelihood). [22]

The Newark Daily Mercury carried similar comments
on Miss Heron and company. In addition, it noted: "for the
first time since our theatre passed from the control of the
late Mrs. Parker, it was last evening honored by the presence of some of our best citizens, who were drawn thither
by the world wide reputation of Miss Matilda Heron. And
well were they repaid, for, in our opinion, no such life-like
acting has ever before been witnessed in our little theatre."[22]

Whether a twentieth century audience would find Miss
Heron's acting "truthful" or "life-like" is highly questionable
Certainly her effort was to present the character as con-
ceived by Dumas fils--a consumptive courtesan. She had
gone to see Mme. Docke in the original Paris production,
studied her work in detail, and had made her own transla-
tion. She did not tamper with the original. Unlike her pred-
ecessor, Miss Jean Davenport, she did not transform the
lady of the camellias into a virginal flirt. Nor did she
pander the public taste, as had Miss Laura Keene, by adding a prologue and epilogue which treated the play as a
dream. As a result Miss Heron's Camille, although contro-
versial, appeared timely and true-to-life. [24]

Matilda Heron's acting seemed to invite intimacy with
unrestrained emotions which some found a "repulsive natural-
ness" (Winter's words) while others, an exciting break with
tradition. Her "first entrance was wonderfully unconven-
tional," said the hero of Fitz-James O'Brien's short story
Mother of Pearl.

The woman dared to come in upon that painted
scene as if it really was the home apartment

> it was represented to be. She did not slide
> in with her face to the audience, and wait
> for the mockery that is called 'a reception.'
> She walked in easily, naturally, unwitting of
> any outside eyes. The petulant manner in
> which she took off her shawl, the common-
> place conversational tone in which she spoke
> to her servant, were revelations . . . .
> Here was a daring reality. Here was a
> woman who, sacrificing for the moment all
> conventional prejudices, dared to play the
> lorette as the lorette herself plays her
> dramatic life . . . .[25]

The Mercury observer was pleased with the performance and its reception. He had no doubt that other stars would follow Miss Heron "and if so we predict a profitable season . . . ."[26] But others did not follow this brief season of seven days. It ended on May 5 with Mr. Loveday and Mr. Charles Foster in the old, but currently meaningful Damon and Pythias.

Free and Easy: The New Idea

For more than two years, from 1862 to 1864, no legitimate drama appeared on the stage of the Newark Theatre. The pleasures of a wartime public were being more conveniently answered by the "Free and Easy" establishments, which appeared to mushroom overnight throughout the city. The Free and Easy provided continuous entertainment of a varied nature with the additional attraction of drinks and food. Undoubtedly they provided a kind of diversion required by a transient military populace and a war-weary community.

On February 27, 1863, the Newark Theatre officially recognized this war-time trend in entertainment. Messrs. Hitchcock and McMannes reopened the Theatre as a "concert

saloon" and found themselves crowded to excess during the
entire evening. Coincidental with this new policy at Newark's first legitimate theater, Miss Laura Keene's Dramatic
Company appeared for one performance at Library Hall. As
an indication of a real shift in public requirements, it should
be noted that this performance (despite a program of light
comedies) was attended by a very small complimentary group
and not at all by a "paying audience." The kind of program
which Concert Saloon was to present with continuing success,
playing nightly to crowded houses, consisted typically of
"laughable" pantomimes, songs and dances, Negro acts and,
periodically, short comedies or musical burlesques. In
November Mr. McMannes became sole manager and the
Concert Saloon became the "New Idea," but the nature of
the program remained old and unchanged. [27]

As the "Casino of the New Idea" (to give its full
name) the Newark Theatre continued as a home for popular
entertainment. C. W. Parker, contortionist and performer
on the flying rings was greeted by an audience of over 1,100
people. His engagement was extended over three weeks in
January 1864. During this time he amazed audiences with
his chair acts, glass acts as well as by packing himself into
a 16 by 20 inch box. Veritably Mr. Parker was the boneless
man. His engagement was followed by the Empire Minstrels
who were featured along with sparring exhibitions, clarinet
soloists, and trick dogs. Thus it went through March. April
found a few single events at the Casino. At the end of the
month (April 29), Concert Hall Theatre was up for sale. [28]
Thus ended the era of "Free and Easy."

Enter Kate Fisher, on Horseback

        At the end of the summer the Advertiser announced
the reopening of the Newark Theatre by G. W. Thompson
for the "lovers of legitimate drama." The lovers of legitimate drama may have been somewhat surprised to discover that the featured performers were Lafayette and
Carlos, two prairie dogs.[29] Despite such disillusionment,
within a few weeks hope must have soared at the announcement that Miss Kate Fisher (with her horse, Wonder) was
reopening the theater on August 24th. For her first
appearance Miss Fisher selected the "horse piece," Mazeppa,
the leading role of which she had recently performed in
New York for thirty nights.[30] Horses are, at any rate,
bigger than dogs.

        Miss Kate Fisher sought, as others had sought be-
fore her, to establish a stock company in Newark. She had
been a rather regular member of the New Bowery Theatre
(New York) from its opening in September, 1859. It is
very likely she envisioned for Newark a bit of the New
Bowery which was (according to the New York Herald of
September 6, 1859) "always full of bustle and gayety at night
[with] knights, heroes, distressed maidens, funny servants
[and] a terrible plot . . . ." Her own success there was
primarily as an equestrienne in such "horse pieces" as Mazeppa and Dick Turpin (Rockwood).[31]

                    Spectacular Beginning
        Mazeppa (which had had a sensational revival at the
New Bowery with Adah Isaacs Menken in 1862) had been one
of the sensations of the old Bowery in the 1830's. At that

time the role of Mazeppa was undertaken by a man, Mr.
Gale, who was (according to the New York Mirror of October
12, 1833) "lashed to the back of his steed [which] dashes up
an awful precipice of some ten feet slantendicular--turns
suddenly and speeds up another ten feet--wheels again, and
up he whirls even to the 'carpenters' gallery . . . ."[32]
Thirty years later at the New Bowery (and possibly at the
Newark Theatre) Miss Fisher was repeating those "terrible
ascents and descents" with the addition of "a flight completely around the first circle of boxes."[33]   And the audience,
thrilled by the daring excitement of romance and adventure,
forgot its cares and returned home pleasantly exhausted.

The Theatre reopened to a crowded house and Mazeppa was accounted a "grand success." It was repeated for
three more performances. Mazeppa was also an "immense"
personal success for Miss Fisher and her horse, Wonder.
She responded by presenting The Three Fast Men or Life in
New York which permitted Newark audiences to see her ver-
satility as she impersonated eight characters and introduced
"all the Gems of Modern and Ancient Minstrelsy." Wonder
joined her in Lightwood and Thunderbolt. [34]

Miss Fisher's company consisted variously of Messrs.
Porter, J. J. Pryor, T. J. Herndon, F. M. Chapman;
Mrs. Jordan and Little Miss Jordan; the Misses Florence
La Fond, C. J. Wallace, Charlotte Richardson, and Miss
Mary Western. Her season reflected the popular taste of
the times with its emphasis upon the spectacular and thrilling
The French Spy, the grand Oriental spectacle of The Cat-
aract of the Ganges, The Female Horse Thief, and the moral
drama Ticket-of-Leave Man might be cited as character-

izing her first season, which lasted until October 3.[35]

The Theater Remodeled

The house, which had enjoyed a run of legitimate
theater for around seven weeks, closed for alterations and
improvements. An article in the Advertiser (September 12,
1864) cited Miss Kate Fisher as "an illustration of what
talent and energy combined will effect. She commenced at
this theatre under the immense difficulties of its having lost
prestige, but she has by her assiduity, by the selection of
a good company, and by the manner in which her pieces are
placed upon the stage, as well as the enforcement of good
order, succeeded in attracting patronage from the best class
. . . ." Perhaps now Newark would have a permanent
theater company. The success of the first season gave Miss
Fisher hope. She reopened the theater as Miss Kate Fisher's
Theatre (H. G. Clarke as Stage Manager) on November 2.
There continued to be a large responsive audience.

Miss Fisher made some significant changes in the
theater. The interior of the building had been not only re-
painted but remodeled as well. Private boxes were added
and the parquette made more pleasant with easy orchestra
chairs. The main entrance to the theater, from Market
Street, led to the parquette and private boxes. Miss Fisher
added a new and separate entrance to the gallery from Harrison (now Halsey) Street. The change of the entrance to
the gallery was considered the greatest improvement because
it obviated "the difficulties and annoyances heretofore experienced." Thus Miss Fisher hoped to attract more of the
fashionable audience and regain prestige. Aside from the

elegance of 150 new orchestra chairs and four "splendid"
private boxes, Miss Fisher had completely new scenery
designed by John Thorne, from Niblo's Garden, New York,
assisted by J. Hilliard. [36]

Kate Fisher Continues

The second season opened with Eustache Baudin and
the laughable farce Mr. and Mrs. White. C. W. Clarke
headed the company of players which, along with Miss Fisher,
he continued to do until Miss Major Pauline Cushman appeared at the end of the month. Miss Fisher began presenting a
more comprehensive season. Star engagements brought
specialty items associated with each visitor. This was
coupled with Miss Fisher's own growing repertoire. The
production of Boucicault's Zoe, The Octoroon [sic] with Miss
Fisher in the title role and Mr. Clarke as Salem Scudder
opened November 11 to a "large and fashionable" audience
which called Miss Fisher to appear before the curtain after
the play. On November 12, Saturday, "hundreds were turned
away from the theatre . . . . So great was the crowd that
standing room only could be attained." The play was Don
Caesar de Bazan, with Mr. Clarke a "decided hit in his
great character." For his benefit a few days later, Mr.
C. W. Clarke was to present his "two best characters, "
Raffaelle de Foix in Raffaelle or The Reprobate of Paris and
Edward Middleton in The Drunkard. The latter character
had been portrayed by Mr. Clarke for over 800 consecutive
nights in New York and was considered "a superior piece of
acting." As Rolla in Pizarro, Mr. Clarke made his last
appearance of a season in which he had presented to Newark

audiences his popular roles. Other than those mentioned,
these included The Corsican Brothers, Captain Kyd, Still
Waters Run Deep, Willow Copse, and John Poole's Cudjo's
Cave, [37] a grouping Odell would very likely have found sound-
ing like a season at New York's Bowery.

Miss Major Pauline Cushman and Associate
        With the appearance of Miss Major Pauline Cushman,
there was another variation in the selection of plays. Miss
Cushman (assisted by the comedian, J. M. Ward) presented
a repertory of Irish plays. She opened her engagement as
Kathleen Kavanaugh in Peep O'Day or Savoureen Deelish,
with Mr. Ward as Barney O'Toole. Miss Cushman was
greeted by a large and appreciative audience and continued to
be so greeted through the week-long run of Peep O'Day. Because of a death in the family Miss Cushman did not appear
for the December 1 performance. She was replaced for that
performance by Miss Jennie Parker, who was featured in the
production which followed, Boucicault's Colleen Bawn. In
the Boucicault play, Miss Cushman played the title role,
Mr. Ward, Miles Na Coppaleen and Miss Parker, Anne
Shute. [38]
        The engagement of Miss Major Pauline Cushman and
Mr. J. M. Ward extended through December 10, according
to the Advertiser. During this time Newarkers saw them
also in such dialect pieces as Ireland and America, The Maid
of Munster with Miss Cushman as Kate O'Brien, and Irish
Assurance and Yankee Modesty. For their benefit on December 9, Miss Cushman and Mr. Ward appeared in Mrs. Fox's
The Ticket-of-Leave Woman. To this performance was add-

ed a special event. Miss Major Pauline Cushman gave the
audience an account of her adventures in the Secret Service
of the United States.

Following Miss Cushman's engagement, Miss Fisher
and company presented Newark John Brougham's Bel- Demonio,
Oliver Twist, Mazeppa (again with Wonder), Ticket- of- Leave
Man, Jack Sheppard, new heaters in the theater and Macbeth coming!

The Year Out and In

The appearance of McKean Buchanan and daughter,
Virginia, was heralded as "the first attempt in this city for
many years to lift the theatrical performances above the lighter styles of dramatic entertainment. "[39] Their production of
Macbeth, which brought back C. W. Clarke as Macduff, was
greeted by "rapturous applause [from those whose] best an-
ticipations were fully realized." The productions of Hamlet,
Richard III, and Othello continued to attract large, fashionable audiences. Following this "lift, " the Newark Theatre
returned to some of its lighter favorites with Dick Turpin
and The French Spy being offered as the Christmas Day
matinee, and Dot or Cricket on the Hearth followed by Mazeppa in the evening. Mr. and Mrs. Gomersal added Waiting
for the Verdict; The Child of the Regiment; and Wallace, the
Hero of Scotland, among others. On Saturday, December 31,
Newark theater- goers saw the old year out with Miss Fisher
playing Maria, Paul, Miss Effie, Molly, and Sally Ann in
The Young American Actress, followed by the 5th act of
Richard III with Miss Fisher as Richard on horseback. Newark theater- goers saw the New Year in with Uncle Tom's

Cabin in the afternoon, and Green Bushes and Dick Turpin
in the evening. [40]   (What happened to Damon and Pythias?
It had become a kind of theatrical doxology.)

Bright Days Ahead

Kate Fisher's Newark Theatre seemed to have established itself as the home of legitimate theater. In the variations in programming, dependent upon the particular stars
engaged, Newark audiences were presented a choice ranging
from the popularly current, through established favorites, to
the classics. The apparent success of legitimate theater,
supported by a fashionable audience, encouraged the reopening of Washington Hall as the Opera House on January 14 for
a season with a variety and minstrel troupe under the direction of J. H. Taylor. The addition of a second theater was
premature. In less than a month the Opera House disappeared along with its troupe and Washington Hall reappeared
with a lecture by an elocutionist. [41]   Kate Fisher's Newark
Theatre, however, continued strong well into spring. During
this time Newarkers saw Miss Addie Kunkel and Miss Fanny
Herring and the return of such favorites as Kate Denin Ryan,
Mr. Neafie, Miss Major Pauline Cushman, again James M.
Ward. Later in the year Mr. Ward was to make his own
efforts for the legitimate theater by becoming lessee and
manager of the Newark Theatre. In the meantime, the first
new attraction of 1865 was Mr. Frank Drew. [42]

Mr. Drew had recently returned from Europe where
he had attained a considerable reputation. Burlesques were
Mr. Drew's forte, among which were Mazeppa or The Fiery
Untamed Rocking Horse and Camille. Mr. Drew had pre-

viously played the character of Mazeppa for over 100 nights
in Mrs. John Woods' theater in New York. His engagement
included Acting Mad, Handy Andy, The Irish Emigrant and
Rip Van Winkle. Following Mr. Drew, Miss Kate Fisher
reappeared on the boards in Dick Turpin on Horseback (with
horse, Wonder), and The French Spy, and Boucicault's The
Streets of New York. On January 12, Miss Fisher received
and took a complimentary benefit, in recognition of her
efforts to establish a first class theater in Newark. On this
occasion Miss Fisher presented the romantic drama Putnam,
The Iron Son of '76, followed by The Rough Diamond. She
was assisted by Mr. James M. Ward. For the next few
weeks Miss Fisher fulfilled engagements in Washington and
Baltimore before returning to Newark on February 8. [43]

While the Rider Is Away

Following Kate Fisher's departure Miss Emma Johnson (who was engaged as the leading actress) and Mr. H. G.
Clarke (stage manager of the theater) appeared in Lady of
Lyons. The next evening they appeared in Willow Copse. On
Monday, January 16, the Advertiser announced the return two-
day engagement of Miss Kate Denin (the Ryan is omitted
this time) and Sam Ryan. Miss Denin starred with Miss
Johnson in East Lynne or The Earl's Daughter. Mr. Ryan
starred in Mountain Outlaw X. Mr. C. W. Clarke also reappeared briefly in his favorite role as Eustache Baudin and
for his benefit next night in Lime Kiln Man, among others.
On January 23, Miss Addie Kunkel appeared in Camille or
The Fate of a Coquette (the Jean Davenport version?). On
succeeding evenings Miss Kunkel appeared in Lady of Lyons,

the protean play of Four Sisters, The Stranger, Bob Nettles,
and All that Glitters Is Not Gold. Cherry and Fair Star was
given six performances in the first week of February with
Miss Kunkel appearing both as star and, apparently for the
interim without Kate, lessee of the Newark Theatre. The
scenery for this production was by J. R. Wilkins, Esq. It
included a Fiery Dragon, Boiling Waters, and Rolling Waters
which were variously "admired by the large and fashionable
audiences."[44]

At the close of Cherry and Fair Star and its scenic
wonders, Miss Kate Fisher returned climactically in nine
different characters. The plays were Three Fast Men and
Nature and Philosophy. They were followed on three succeeding evenings by Streets of New York; Nan, The Good
for Nothing; Dick Turpin; and Putnam, The Iron Son of '76.
Although he is not specifically mentioned, Wonder undoubtedly continued his popular supporting role in at least two of
the aforementioned. (Elsewhere in Newark, Father Kemp's
Old Folks were competing with Brother Jonathan's Old
Folks; Morris and Wilson's Minstrels were to compete with
Sam Sharpley's Minstrels, in between which events was
Sneezing Jed Perkins.)[45]

Stars, Cues, and Portents

In the next two weeks the Newark Theatre offered the
separate engagements of Mr. Neafie and Miss Fanny Herring.
Mr. Neafie's return also marked the return of Shakespeare
to the Newark boards (and brought some criticism of the
company). Mr. Neafie's opening production was Macbeth,
with Locke's vocal and instrumental music. It was announced

that the witch scenes would be presented by the whole company. Variations and adaptations of Shakespeare being usual,
there was no adverse criticism from purists. Mr. Neafie's
Macbeth was "successful." A few days later he was "a
great success" in Hamlet. Other than for those portraying
Ophelia, Polonius, and the Gravedigger, the rest of the company received a critical scolding for being ignorant of their
parts and having to be prompted. Miss Western was informed that she would have "done better to carry her book and
read her role." Mr. Neafie continued to be a personal
success as Ruy Blas, Don Caesar de Bazan, and Richard III
while his supporting cast continued to be ill-prepared. [46]

On February 20, Miss Fanny Herring made her first
appearance in Newark. For her opening gambit she portrayed six different characters in Satan in Paris or The Mysterious Stranger, followed by Loan of a Lover. On the next
evening Miss Herring presented (for the first time in Newark) Lysiah, The Abandoned by Charles Smith Cheitham,
Esq. [47.] Lysiah was, according to Odell, "as near to Leah,
The Forsaken as the law permitted them to go." It had
played for three weeks of "profitable abandoning" in October,
1864, at Fox's Old Bowery where, the New York Herald
noted "Miss Fanny Herring is the great attraction at this
house." The writer notes further along "it does not take
much to make a sensation in the Old Bowery . . . . the broad
wit and strong dramatic incidence of the Bowery stage are a
success as profitable to the management as it is satisfactory
to the audience." [48] Since the typical fare of the Newark
Theatre was similar to the typical offerings of the Old and
New Bowery Theatres, one might assume profitable success

to the Newark management also.   At any rate, the present
season continued unbroken into April.

Repeats, Adds, and Drops

        The summer season brought back some Newark favor-
ites, a new play for Miss Fisher, and some changes in the
company.   Miss Major Pauline Cushman and the Irish comedian, Mr. James M. Ward, returned on March 6 in Peep
O'Day and Barney, The Baron.   They were greeted by one
of the largest houses of the season, which Mr. Ward, in
particular, kept in "roars of laughter."   Mr. Neafie returned also on March 20 with substantially the same program of
plays he had offered little more than a month earlier.
Miss Kate Fisher, however, introduced on March 13 "for the
first time in Newark" Rosina Meadows or Temptations Unveiled with herself in the title role.[49]   Miss Fisher also
made some changes in the company, adding new people and
dropping others.   Among the latter were Mr. W. H. Bloom-
field and Miss Mary Western, who apparently still had trouble
"getting off book."   despite these changes, Mr. Neafie's problem of an ill-prepared supporting cast remained.   He, nonetheless, continued to draw large houses.   Newark had its
favorite actor, if not its favorite company.

        Once more we move into dark days in the life of the
Newark Theatre.   Cultural events are again typified by a
few lectures and scattered appearances of musical varieties
by such groups as the Alleghenians and Swiss Bell Ringers.
A local dramatic association emerged, however, which was
named for the favorite son and visitor, Mr. Neafie.   There
was, perhaps, a portent of the golden days to come when

Mr. James M. Ward attempted to reintroduce a permanent
company in Newark. The Theatre was rechristened the Ward
Theatre and as such reopened on May 14, 1866. Mr. Ward's
season ran somewhat erratically into the middle of June. On
June 14, 1866, the Advertiser noted improvements at Concert Hall, otherwise known as the Newark Theatre. The
proprietor "intends to shortly, completely remodel the interior of the establishment . . . ." The wave of hope was
still high. Miss Kate Fisher left but not without accomplishment. Perhaps her efforts had prepared the way for a new
era--another reign of gold.

Notes

1.   Pierson, Narratives of Newark (Newark: Pierson
             Publishing Co., 1917), p. 274, 278, 280.

2.   Pierson's Newark City Directory 1858-1859 (Newark:
             B. F. Pierson, 1859); cf 1860 Essex County
             (U. S. Census), p. 98, 875.

3.   Newark Daily Advertiser (January 3, 1860).

4.   Ibid. for periods indicated.

5.   See p. 85.

6.   Lloyd Morris, Curtain Time (New York: Random House
             Inc., 1953), p. 192, 199.

7.   Barnard Hewitt, Theatre U. S. A.: 1668 to 1957
             (New York: McGraw-Hill, 1959), p. 187.

8.   George C. D. Odell, Annals of the New York Stage,
             VII (New York: Columbia University Press, 1931),
             p. 388; Oral S. Coad and Edwin Mims, Jr.,
             "The American Stage," The Pageant of America
             (New Haven: Yale University Press, 1929),
             Vol. XIV, p. 191.

9.   Newark Daily Advertiser (August 31- September 12,
             1861).

10.   Odell, Annals, VII, p. 108, 404.

11.   Newark Daily Advertiser, for dates indicated; also
       Odell, Annals, VII, p. 452.

12.   E. J. West, "Revolution in the American Theatre,"
       Theatre Survey, I (1960), p. 48, 49.

13.   Newark Daily Advertiser (November 18-30, 1861).

14.   Ibid. (December 2-26, 1861).

15.   Odell, Annals, VII, p. 138.

16.   Newark Daily Advertiser (December 9-23, 1861).

17.   Ibid. (March 1-3, 1862).

18.   Ibid. (March, 1862).

19.   Ibid. (April 21, 1862).

20.   Ibid. (April 28, 30, 1862).

21.   Ibid. (April 29, 1862).

22.   Ibid. (April 30, 1862).

23.   Newark Daily Mercury (April 29, 1862).

24.   West, "Revolution in the American Theatre," p. 47-
       48.

25.   Quoted in Hewitt, Theatre U. S. A., p. 183.

26.   Newark Daily Mercury (April 30, 1862).

27.   See Newark Daily Advertiser (February 27, 1863),
       and succeeding issues for specific events during
       this period.

28.   Ibid., and succeeding issues for this period.

29.   Ibid. (June 30, 1864).

30.   Ibid. (August 19, 1864).

31.   Odell, Annals, VII, p. 236-237, 571.

32.   Quoted in Hewitt, Theatre U. S. A., p. 117-18.

33.   Odell, Annals, VII, p. 570-71.

34.   Newark Daily Advertiser (August 24-September 3,
       1864).

35.   Ibid. (September 1-October 3, 1864).

36.   Ibid. (November 3, 1864).

37.   Ibid.   (November 2-26, 1864).   All quoted matter
          in this paragraph may be attributed to this source.

38.   Ibid.   (November 28-December 7, 1864).

39.   Newark Daily Advertiser (December 17, 1864).

40.   Ibid.   (December 19-31, 1864).

41.   Ibid.   (January 14-February 1, 1865).

42.   Ibid.   (January 3, 1865).

43.   Ibid.   (January 3-12, 1865).

44.   Ibid.   (January 16-February 7, 1865).

45.   Ibid.   (February 8-11, 1865).

46.   Ibid.   (February 13-18, 1865).

47.   Ibid.   (February 20-22, 1865).

48.   Odell, Annals, VII, p. 654.

49.   Miss Fisher is not counting the performance of
          Mrs. Amelia Parker seven years earlier.   See
          Appendix B.

Chapter V

Of Gold Again and a New Era

November 8, 1866, may be set down as the "inauguration of a New Era of the Drama" in Newark. [1] Although the new era was short lived, it remains a golden moment, indeed the last significant period in the efforts to establish a permanent stock company in Newark. Very shortly the concept of the stock company disappeared, being replaced by the more economically secure touring company. Concert Hall, which, since its inception in 1847, had been the scene of various efforts, survived the change. Almost twenty years later, the boards on which Charlotte Barnes had trod and received acclaim as the "people's favorite" supported the "remarkable powers" of Emma Waller, whom William Winter called "a tragic actress of the first rank . . . ." [2] Emma Waller, and her husband Daniel Wilmarth Waller, leased the theater and during the summer had it rebuilt and remodeled in preparation for the "New Era."

Mr. Waller, who came from Paterson "with high testimonials," employed an impressive array of artists and craftsmen to completely rebuild and remodel the interior of the theater

> in every department, and the most extensive and various additions and improvements that experience could suggest for the comfort and convenience of the auditors have been signally effected. Perfect ventilation has been secured by all of the most recent suggestions that science could devise. The entire building will be comfortably heated at all times, thus rendering

it, as regards ventilation and temperature, one of the most agreeable and comfortable establishment in the Union.

New scenery was created by Messrs. L. W. Seavey, J. Hillard, Jr., and S. Culbert to be handled by machinery devised by Messrs. Thomas Morgan and L. Sandford. The house boasted frescoes by Mr. Albert Metz of Newark and was lighted by gas which utilized Frink's Patent Reflectors. [3]

The Dramatic Company was especially selected from theaters in New York, Philadelphia, and Boston "with the view of giving dignity and tone to the Drama in this city...." It consisted of

Mrs. Emma Waller,

Mr. F. G. Gossin,   Mr. Joseph Barrett,
Mr. W. S. Higgins,   Mr. W. D. Shiels,
Mr. G. W. Harrison,   Mr. G. H. Maxwell,
Mr. J. C. Walsh,   Mr. Thos. Martin,
Mr. John Morton,   Mr. J. N. Dres,
Mr. John Stanley,   Mr. G. W. Shields,

[and]

Mrs. Viola Barrett,   Mrs. Eliza LeBrun,
Miss Blanche Maravia,   Miss Viola Plunkett,
Miss Alice Cole,   Miss Kate Cole,

Miss Virginia LeBrun

The orchestra, "selected with great care," was under the direction of Professor Anton Zilm. Boucicault's London Assurance was announced as the opening production. [4] All in all, everything was ready for the "New Era," and, not inappropriately, the theater was rechristened Waller's Opera House.

Curtain Rises

The opening night audience was greater than could be

seated. At the beginning they choked the aisles, presenting
some initial embarrassment to Mr. Waller, but undoubtedly
providing much more delight. As many hardy, persistent
souls as could be accomodated were permitted to stand. At
approximately seven thirty, Professor Zilm mounted the
podium and the orchestra played the "Star-Spangled Banner";
the company, led by Mrs. Barrett, sang in chorus. Following this, the gas lights dimmed and the grand drapery opened,
revealing magnificent gold and damask furniture (imported from Paris) in front of the bright new settings. The actors appeared in rich and apparently costly costumes. Soon
Mrs. Emma Waller, as Lady Gay Spanker, made her first
appearnace in Newark. Although there was a certain stiff-
ness on the part of a few actors, it was apparent that the
play was well-rehearsed and the parts well studied, for there
was no noticeable prompting whatsoever. London Assurance,
"with its powerful and efficient cast, splendid appointments
and charming mise-en-scene," played for three successful
evenings, hopefully suggesting what one might call a kind of
Newark assurance to the Wallers for the season to come. [5]

Boucicault's play met with continuing success. The
next week Waller's Opera House presented in quick succession a different production each night. These included the
standard English dramas such as The Stranger, The Hunchback, The Lady of Lyons, and The School for Scandal. A
local critic noted the "remarkable determination and success
thus far [of] the opening promises of this undertaking." [6]
Greatly impressed with the quality of the company, despite
their being "overworked" by the quick succession of productions, our critic further noted (the next week) that the compa-

ny performed "with a personal interest and zest which is a
condition to success not always manifested on such occasions,
and the absence of that crudeness which usually mars a first
effort in new parts, proved the carefullness of their study."[7]
This was in marked contrast to the criticism variously directed to the Kate Fisher Company. It also spoke well not only
for Mr. Waller's management but more particularly of Mrs.
Emma Waller's direction.

The Queen: Emma Waller, With Consort

     English born Mrs. Emma Waller had made her first
London appearance at Drury Lane in 1856, as Pauline in The
Lady of Lyons. She played Ophelia in Philadelphia on October 19, 1857, and made her New York debut, with her husband, as Marina in The Duchess of Malfi on April 5, 1858,
at the Broadway.[8] Odell records Mrs. Waller as "an admirable actress . . . [who along with her husband] received
cordial critical recognition, but their engagement was not
profitable."[9] Following this, aside from an appearance on
May 16, 1864, Mrs. Waller was absent from the New York
stage until December 27, 1869. For her reappearance in
New York--at the Booth--Mrs. Waller selected the role of
Meg Merrilies in Guy Mannering and gave what Winter
has called "one of the most powerful performances that have
been seen in our time."[10] More than three years before
this brilliant New York coup, Mrs. Waller had presented at
the Newark Theatre the characterization for which she was to
gain a reputation which rivaled that of Charlotte Cushman.
She presented Guy Mannering for four performances at Waller's Opera House beginning November 19, 1865.[11]

As Meg Merrilies, Mrs. Waller "justified the compliments she has received," according to the observer for the Newark Daily Advertiser, "and all together gave a vivid impersonation of that terrible gipsey [sic] whom Scott has made memorable."[12] William Winter gives us a description of Mrs. Waller as Meg Merrilies.

> The wasted face, the blazing eyes, the rigid muscles, the bony fingers, the wild hair, the wretched garments, they were all signs of a hard life, tokens of want and misery, pathetically indicative of that disordered reason . . . which yet is iron true to one distinct and righteous purpose. The weird dignity of her bearing was impressive beyond words; they were moments, indeed, when she seemed to be a soul inspired by communion with beings of another world. Her acting, in the strange reverie in which Meg Merrilies sings the cradle song to Bertram, was overwhelming in its pathos: the light of madness seemed to fade out of her eyes, giving place to all the woman-like sweetness of gentle, loving, happy youth. Nothing in the world is more desolate than the irremediable misery of age, and there never was a better type than Mrs. Waller's Meg Merrilies of the anguish of a breaking mind, that looks back to youth and happiness from among its own ruins . . . . Her death-scene as Meg, notwithstanding that it included a delineation of physical agony, was in no particular common, it inspired awe and sorrow; and, in this representative dramatic passage, as in many a kindred one, by the excitation of terror and pity the actress accomplished the true purpose of tragedy and left her hearers chastened, ennobled, and subdued. The Stage ought never to forget her example.[13]

Guy Mannering was followed by one performance on November 23 of Camille and on November 24 of Lucretia Borgia with Mrs. Waller in the title roles. At this point Mrs. Waller took a respite from the additional demands of

acting to devote herself to directorial matters. The company next presented Uncle Tom's Cabin. It played to full
houses for three evenings and the Daily Advertiser reported
"it was evident from the interest it excited [that] · · · popular sympathy [was] . . . still fresh." It seemed evident
also that Waller's Opera House was answering the need for
legitimate theater in Newark. After three weeks of operation the management announced that they had added eighty
more "sittings" to the reserve section of the house. [14]

Emma Waller reappeared in the second of what were
called her "characteristic, best, and most admirable performances," [15] on December 8. She acted Lady Macbeth to her
husband's portrayal of the title role. Daniel Wilmarth Waller had been conspicuous from the very beginning as a name
on programs and advertisements but his person had been concealed behind the scenes. He made his first appearance in
Newark as an actor on December 6, in the role of Hamlet
which he did "quite well." The Thursday night house for
Hamlet was fair but hardly full. A large audience, however,
greeted the appearance of both the Wallers together on Saturday as Macbeth and his Lady. A local observer, impressed
with their performances, was nonetheless surprised that they
would venture on the boards at all what with all their duties
of management. [16]

The duties of management notwithstanding, Emma
Waller apparently found time in addition for playwriting.
She appeared next in "her new original play," Naomi, The
Deserted (also referred to as The Curse of Naomi). [17] The
Newark newspapers made no comment on Naomi other than
to note that it was to be repeated. Otherwise it was dropped

from the company's repertoire, and seems not to have
followed Mrs. Waller into her later New York successes.
Of Mrs. Emma Waller as playwright, history records only
that her new original play was given two performances in
Newark with herself in the title role.

Managerial duties undoubtedly required the greater
part of D. W. Waller's time. Although he began his professional career as an actor, and is remembered chiefly in
this capacity, Mr. Waller devoted himself to establishing
Waller's Opera House in Newark and to promoting the talents
of his wife. Every three or four months, however, during
their sojourn in Newark, he made one or two appearances
on the stage with Mrs. Waller. At these times they usually
presented Macbeth, Othello, The Stranger, The Sicilian
Pirate, or The Duchess of Malfi. Mr. Waller was considered "a natural, judicious, original actor" whose reading was
always "in accordance with the spirit of the lines. His voice
was full, clear and flexible--in the lower register singular-
ly melodious and powerful."[18]

Part of his judiciousness lay also in promoting Mrs.
Waller. T. A. Brown reaffirms that she "was a great actress. She grasped all the elements which make up a
character, and ruled them with rare power. The great
charm of her acting was that she always kept the actress
in the background when placing her characters on the stage.
Her Lady Macbeth was a wonderful performance, and I
doubt if its equal has ever been seen on the American
stage."[19] Of the performances Mr. and Mrs. Waller gave
together, the Newark presses (always frustratingly spare in
critical observations) offer us no insight. They found Mr.

Waller's Othello "a decided improvement of his former [e.g.,
Hamlet, Macbeth] characters." Of Mrs. Waller's portrayal
of Iago they noted that she appeared as well " in the part as
was possible of one of her sex," the nature of Iago being
"foreign to every female instinct . . . ."20 We are afforded no critical comments on their presentation of The Duchess
of Malfi, although Winter considers that to be the third of
Mrs. Emma Waller's great characterizations.

With the holidays approaching, Waller's Opera House
presented a change of program with the engagements of the
Worrell sisters and T. L. Donnelly, followed the next week
by the comedian Stuart Robson. A local observer noted that
"the theatre going public are evidently more strongly inclined
just now for the lighter performances which please the eye
and touch the fancy, than by legitimate drama which demands
an intellectual effort."21 These lighter performances, which
were mounted with a "beautiful style," consisted primarily
of fairy burlesques such as Cinderella, The Invisible Queen,
Fra Diavalo and The Elves or The Statue Bride along with
such comic burlesques as Mazeppa or The Untamed Rocking
Horse, King Lear, The Cuss and the romantic Forty Thieves
or The Wood-Cutters of Bagdad. The lighter program met
with gratifying public response. For the December 25 performance there was a "perfect jam . . . and the aisles and
lobbies as well as the seats were overflowing." The management re-engaged Mr. Robson for another week, extending
into January, 1867. Among the new burlesques he presented
during this time were Hamlet or The Wearing of the Black
and Camille or The Cracked Heart.22

Visiting Royalty

　　With the introduction of this change of pace in programming, the traditional stock pattern of visiting stars was
re-established.　No matter how fine the resident company
may be (and Waller's Opera House seemed not only to have
a very fine company, but was blessed with an outstanding
resident star as well), the public apparently required great
variety and, more particularly, new faces.　Then, as now,
the new face should have publicity value.　During 1867,
Waller's Opera House presented some of the famous and near-
famous performers of the day: E. L. Davenport, J. Albaugh,
Mary Mitchell (sister of the famous Maggie), the beautiful
Rose Eytinge, the enduring Mr. and Mrs. Barney Williams,
Mlle. Lotta, Helen Western and her husband James A.
Hearne, Lady Don (fresh from her New York theater debut),
Kate Reignolds, Joseph Proctor, Mrs. G. C. Howard (the
perennial "Topsy"), Marietta Ravel, Newark's own James M.
Ward (without Miss Capt. Pauline) and Mr. Neafie.　Inter-
spersed among the engagements of these were brief engage-
ments by Emma Waller alone or with her husband.

The Old Order and Transition

　　John E. Owens was the first star in January to follow
Stuart Robson.　Although a native star, Mr. Owens had
recently been approved by English audiences.　Newark audiences were treated to his "new and greatly improved
version of Solon Shingle, which considerably changed the
characters and motivation, and eliminated much of the child-
ish material of the earlier play, The People's Lawyer."[23]
Tickets went on sale well in advance for Mr. Owens' engage-

ment, and many were turned away from the "overflowing
house." Mr. Owens' original three night engagement was
so successful that it was extended to the end of the week,
which necessitated his getting a release from his scheduled
appearance in Cincinnati. [24]

Snow prevented E. L. Davenport from appearing on
January 21. The company presented Ticket- of- Leave Man
in this emergency to "general satisfaction." By the next
day, however, Mr. Davenport had reached Newark and the
local theater-goer saw this eminent actor in Hamlet. It
does not speak well for the community that along with the
announcement of Hamlet Mr. Waller felt it necessary to em-
phasize that he was endeavoring to make arrangements with
other popular stars. One feels that Mr. Waller is re-
assuring the public that such intellectual dramas as Hamlet
are not to be a new trend. As a matter of fact, the only
trend to be associated with the appearance of E. L. Davenport was that of quality and variety. His program in Newark offered the public the opportunity to see him in several
of his outstanding roles ranging from Hamlet through St.
Marc, The Soldier of Fortune to Black-Eyed Susan and Anna
Cora Mowatt's Fashion. His repertoire met with success in
Newark, his St. Marc receiving three curtain calls. [25] A
gifted, versatile actor--one must query along with Odell as
to why he "never quite attained the position on the American
stage for which his great talents seemed to qualify him." [26]

Mary Mitchell followed Mr. Davenport in a dramatization of Dickens' Our Mutual Friend. She brought with
her the "young artist," J. Albaugh. [27] (Then or later Mary
Mitchell was in reality Mrs. Albaugh.) The possibility not-

withstanding, Mitchell seemed to be following a pattern much
on the increase at this period, that of stars bringing with
them at least one or two supporting players, and sometimes
practically whole companies. This innovation, exemplified
also by Miss Major Pauline Cushman and James M. Ward
before he reached independent status and by Mary's sister
Maggie Mitchell and J. W. Collier, was further evidenced
in Newark with the handsome Mrs. D. P. Bowers and J. C.
McCollom (in, among others, her most popular play, Lady
Audley's Secret) and by Miss Helen Western and her husband
James A. Hearne, the future playwright of the "realistic
drama," Margaret Fleming. Stars being accompanied by
supporting players may well have been as Odell suggests,
"the entering wedge for the destruction of the stock system"[28]
and the beginning of the touring companies.

Aside from those stars such as Mr. and Mrs. Williams
whose fame and popularity was as a team, there were still
those individual stars who performed with the existing stock
company. Such a luminary was Rose Eytinge. The New
York Herald of March 29 pronounced on the occasion of her
first appearance at Niblo's in 1864, that Miss Eytinge was
a "young lady of rare personal attraction and unquestionable
promise as an actress." She had joined the Wallack-Davenport team (which had brought its brilliance to Newark in
December, 1861) in June of 1865. Of the Eytinge-Wallack-
Davenport combination the New York Times found it "difficult
to speak without exaggeration. Three such artists on the
stage in any one scene . . . must necessarily lead to
decided results . . . . We recall the entire evening's performance with amazement . . . ."[29] This combination had

gone on to brighten the 1865-66 season at Wallack's Theatre.
It was by no means a slight to her abilities as an actress
that references to Miss Eytinge were generally preceded by
the adjective "beautiful," for her talents were amply recognized in the press.   Miss Eytinge brought two new plays to
the Newark stage: Augustin Daly's dramatization of Charles
Reade's novel Griffith Gaunt or Jealousy and his free adap-
tation from Sardou's Nos Bons Villageois entitled Hazardous
Ground.   The former had been presented with success at the
New York Theatre on November 7, 1866, with Miss Eytinge
creating the role of Kate Peyton.   For a verbal picture of
Miss Eytinge in this role we must turn elsewhere than to the
Newark Presses, typically lacking in critical evaluation of
performances.   Speaking of the New York Theatre produc-
tion, the Times of November 12 reports:

> Miss Rose Eytinge plays the part to perfec-
> tion.   The "grand and beautiful orbs" of the
> original Kate did not surpass those of her
> American representative.   In the entire con-
> ception of the character, Miss Eytinge dis-
> plays the well-read and cultured artist; the
> actress who has studied not only her lines
> and the necessary business that they involve,
> but the full intent and scope of the author's
> meaning . . . . Miss Eytinge's style in
> repose is eminently natural and unconcerned;
> in excitement it is defiant, sacrificial but not
> violent . . . . We have long considered Miss
> Eytinge the leading actress of the American
> stage, and our readers will share the opinion
> with us after witnessing her performance of the
> difficult and, in some respects, embarrassing
> role of Kate Peyton. [30]

A few months later Miss Kate Reignolds was to make
her Newark debut in the same role.   History affords us no
basis for comparison of Miss Reignolds in the role.   For our

verbal portrait of Miss Reignolds we turn again to William
Winter, writing in the New York Tribune on November 28,
1866: "Miss Reignolds always comes hither like a sunbeam.
Grace, elegance, vivacity, the true spirit of laughing mischief,
and withal a vein of earnest and tender sentiment, underlying
archness and glitter, mete and blend in her temperament, and
her manner . . . . She has the rare faculty of fully yielding
her mind to that brilliant, reckless spirit of innocent devil-
try, so to speak, which is the life of much of the old English
comedy." What with such dramas as Griffith Gaunt, Armadale, Lioness of the North, and Lady of Lyons, Miss Reignolds had little opportunity to present "the true spirit of
laughing mischief" to the Newark theater-goer, except in the
comedietta Antony and Cleopatra which she offered as an
after-piece on May 9 and 11.[31]

The New Vivacity

We note that "vivacity" had become the keynote and
basic attribute assigned to the popular new actresses. Of
these "fairy artistes" perhaps the most popular and enduring
was Charlotte (later Carlotta) Crabtree, publicly known as
Lotta. This West Coast phenomenon had made a brief New
York appearance in 1864 at Niblo's Saloon where her banjo
playing, dancing and ready repartee brought vehement shouts
and stamps from the young gentlemen present.[32] Her "debut"
in the East did not take place, however, until July of 1867
at Wallack's Theatre. At that time she appeared as Paul
in The Pet of the Petticoats and as Liddy in Family Jars.
The New York Times of July 30 described her as small,
rather slight in figure, very fair, with a delicate nose and

bright brown eyes. She had "a habit of wreathing her lip,
cheek and brow into a smile of wicked glee . . . . The
character of Paul . . . calls for exactly these character-
istics . . . ." Another reviewer informed us that "Lotta
can be described only by simile . . . . She has been
called 'sunbeam,' a 'cataract,' a 'doll,' a 'kitten,' a
'canary-bird,' a 'volcano,' an 'isle of light,' a 'sparkling
ingot . . . .' What is she? I'll tell you first what she
is not; she is not an actress." In the role of Paul (he
continued) she was "the picture of a yellow-haired, rosy-
cheeked, dark-eyed little darling of its mother. Her snowy-
white pants, braced with starch, hung just low enough to
reveal a very pretty foot . . . and a neatly-turned ankle."[33]
It was with a foot and ankle thrust beyond the curtain and
wriggled at the audience that Lotta made her curtain calls. [34]

     Three months prior to this New York debut Lotta
brought her talents to Waller's Opera House for an engagement of seven performances, cut short when she caught a
cold. At Waller's she had opened her engagement also with
The Pet of the Petticoats. Her Newark repertoire included
Family Jars, Nan the Good for Nothing, The Female Detective and Fanchon the Cricket. [35] This last play was a standard in the repertoire of Maggie Mitchell, for whom the role
seemed tailored. For Lotta, new works were also to be
especially created while old works, according to Hewitt,
were "strained and stretched to permit her to dance, sing,
and play the banjo . . . ."[36]

Intermission
     The dramatic company ended its first season at

Waller's Opera House on May 17, 1867. This also marked
the last night in the engagement of Mr. Joseph Proctor. The
notice that the theater was closing for the summer brought
forth a request from many gentlemen from the city for the
opportunity to "testify their appreciation of . . .[the Waller's]
successful efforts to maintain in this city a first class dramatic establishment in which the attractions have been unim-
paired by the objectionable accompaniments which have de-
moralized the stage elsewhere." The request was for a
Grand Complimentary Benefit. The gentlemen further suggested that for this occasion the price of admission be
raised to one dollar for any place in the house, "not doubt-
ing that it will be filled at that price." Although the Wallers
had apparently earned "the respect and esteem of the best
friends of drama" and had achieved a season of artistic
success, their efforts could hardly be said to have brought
them "pecuniary success."[37]

The Complimentary Benefit was presented on Monday,
May 20. It consisted of The Hunchback with Mrs. Emma
Waller playing Julia and Mr. D. W. Waller playing Master
Walter, and Perfection or The Maid of Munster with Mrs.
Waller as Kate O'Brien. One of the largest audiences of
the season assembled to indicate to Mr. and Mrs. Waller
that they had "fully redeemed the promise they made at the
commencement of their undertaking . . . ." Following the
performance the Wallers were called in front of the curtain
and briefly acknowledged their ovation.[38]

The dramatic season had closed for the summer but
Waller's Opera House remained available for rental by the
night or week until September 1, "for any respectable enter-

tainment, not theatrical."[39]   In general the summer in Newark was culturally lean.   Library Hall had its scattered
lectures, concerts, and exhibitions.   The few "respectable
entertainments" which availed themselves of the "elegant and
commodious" Waller's Opera House consisted of the Imperial
Japanese Troupe (of acrobatic jugglers) in June and again in
July, at which time Litte All Right joined them as star.
Skiff and Gaylord's Minstrels and Morris Brothers' Minstrels
and Brass Band gave two performances each in June and
July respectively.   Perhaps it was the success of the Japanese acrobatic jugglers earlier that prompted Sam Colyer
and his sons to give "some wonderful athletic exhibitions" in
August.   An organ concert followed them two days later.
Then on August 28, a grand olio entertainment was present-
ed as a farewell benefit to Mrs. Viola Barrett.   Since the
entertainment consisted of singing and readings, it apparently fitted the "not theatrical" stipulation regarding use of the
house.   The performers, however, were volunteers from
Wallack's and other New York theaters and included the
Queen sisters and Messrs. D. E. Ralton, Lewis Mestayer,
A. Sedgwick, J. L. Davis, Joseph Barrett, A. Queen and
W. Ellerton.[40]   Mrs. Barrett had been a popular member
of the Newark stock company during its first season.   Her
farewell benefit was obviously quite belated.

Final Curtain

        After the summer's intermission Waller's Opera House
began its second season on Saturday, September 28.   Although the season may have begun amid high hopes, it lasted only ten weeks.   The company gave its final performance,

a benefit for the management, on Monday, December 2.
The fact that the season was not extended for just a few
weeks into the more lucrative holiday period suggests the
degree of despair (both financial and psychological) the
Wallers had for the life of theater in Newark.   Despite the
fact that the first season had "passed without a blunder" and
that the theater-going public in Newark had become "very
much enlarged" through the efforts of the Wallers, the
second season was short-lived.   It had opened with Mr. and
Mrs. Waller in Macbeth and had closed with them in (perhaps
somewhat facetiously) The Honeymoon (now over certainly)
and Dead Shot. [41]   By some strange coincidence, The Honeymoon, which was the last production by the stock company in
1867, was also the first production presented in the Theatre
in Newark, Concert Hall, in 1847.

Curtain Call
        With the Wallers' final performance the "New Era"
had ended.   This conclusion remains, however, a point of
view.   Certainly the hopes of a people in the wake of a
civil war would be revived, for such a period seems always
ripe for accomplishment.   For Mr. and Mrs. D. W. Waller,
the establishment of a fine, disciplined stock company, form-
ing a cultural nucleus for the city of Newark, had been the
goal.   Their goal was not reached.   They presented a well-
managed house in which Newark saw some of the best acting
of the day, often players in roles in which they were yet to
be acclaimed by New York; but a permanent stock company
had not been established.   For them, then, the "New Era"
was a disappointment and hardly new at all--history abounds

with records of the failures of ventures.

It was, nevertheless, a "New Era." The Wallers
had been correct when they proclaimed it, but whereas their
intent (not unlike others in the Nation) was to start again,
re-build, reconstruct what had been, the real "New Era" was
one of change--revolutionary change in the theater--and a
break from what had been. The failure of Waller's Opera
House, with its excellent management and company, affords
us no basis for criticism of either the Wallers or the Newark
public. The Wallers had selected the wrong moment in history. Although the time did not conspire for them, it gives
us the necessary perspective for understanding that which
they could not know or foresee. The old order, the old
school, the old system were not to be re-established in 1867.
As E. J. West informs us: "The movement toward realism,
the pursuit of the profitable long run, the substitution of
the touring companies for the old coalition of the resident
stock company and the visiting star, all were at least accepted, not simply anticipated, by 1870, when the new school
came of age . . . ."[42]

Although the fashions, styles and methods of theater
were to change, the building on the corner of Market and
(now) Halsey Streets would endure into the second decade of
the twentieth century. For awhile it was the Opera House
(Waller's having been dropped), then back to Newark Theatre,
until Fred Waldmann acquired the building in the eighties
and changed the name to Waldmann's Opera House. By that
time, Newark had another theater, the Park, followed
immediately by a third, the Grand Opera House. By 1886,
there were five theaters operating in Newark, with more to

come.   Stars and touring companies continued to play in
Newark.   The familiar names persisted.   New ones were
added: Fanny Janauschek, Addie Ristori, Edwin Booth, Ada
Rehan (making her first appearance on any stage), Lester
Wallack, E. H. Sothern, Julia Marlowe, Ethel Barrymore--
and so goes the list of luminaries.   Gone was the glory
of stock, star, and repertory, but with the close of one
discernible period in the history of theater in Newark, another "New Era" waited in the wings for its entrance cue.

Notes

1.   *Newark Daily Advertiser* (November 5, 1866).

2.   William Winter, *Wallet of Time* (New York: Moffat,
      Yard and Company, 1913), I, p. 194.

3.   *Newark Daily Advertiser* (November 5, 1866).

4.   *Ibid.* (November 6, 1866).

5.   *Ibid.* (November 6-10, 1866).

6.   *Ibid.* (November 15, 1866).

7.   *Ibid.* (November 20, 1866).

8.   Winter, *Wallet of Time,* I, p. 194.

9.   George C. D. Odell, *Annals of the New York Stage*
      (New York: Columbia University Press, 1931), VII,
      p. 194.

10. Winter, *Wallet of Time,* I, p. 196.

11. *Newark Daily Advertiser* (November 19, 1866).

12. *Ibid.* (November 20, 1866).

13. Winter, *Wallet of Time,* I, p. 196-97.

14. *Newark Daily Advertiser* (November 23-28, 1866).

15. Winter, *Wallet of Time,* I, p. 196.

16. *Newark Daily Advertiser* (December 6-10, 1866).

17. *Ibid.* (December 10, 1866).

18.   T. A. Brown, History of the New York Stage
        (New York: Dodd, Mead, 1903), I, p. 409.

19.   Ibid.

20.   Newark Daily Advertiser (December 14, 1866).

21.   Ibid. (December 20, 1866).

22.   Ibid. (December 21, 1866-January 7, 1867).

23.   Odell, Annals of the New York Stage (1936), VIII,
        p. 33.

24.   Newark Daily Advertiser (January 10-16, 1867).

25.   Ibid. (January 21-26, 1867).

26.   Odell, Annals, VIII, p. 3.

27.   Newark Daily Advertiser (January 26, 1867).

28.   Odell, Annals, VIII, p. 145.

29.   Ibid., VII, p. 562, 631.

30.   Ibid., VIII, 7, 183.

31.   Newark Daily Advertiser (May 9, 10, 1867).

32.   Odell, Annals, VII, p. 606.

33.   Barnard Hewitt, Theatre U. S. A.: 1668 to 1957 (New
        York: McGraw Hill, 1959), p. 203, 204.

34.   Lloyd Morris, Curtain Time, (New York: Random
        House, Inc., 1953).

35.   Newark Daily Advertiser (April 16-23, 1867).

36.   Hewitt, Theatre U. S. A., p. 205.

37.   Newark Daily Advertiser (May 18, 1867).

38.   Ibid. (May 21, 1867).

39.   Ibid. (May 27, 1867).

40.   Ibid. Newark Daily Advertiser (May 22-August 28, 1867)

41.   Ibid. (September 26, 28, December 2, 1867).

42.   E. J. West, "Revolution in the American Theatre,"
        Theatre Survey, I (1960), p. 61.

Afterword

The history of the early Newark theater is the story of a theater trying to find its role in the life of a growing, culturally inter-mixed, industrial center. It is also the story of a theater born too late. Urquhart, in his History of the City of Newark, tells us that "the drama has always had more or less difficulty in Newark and the position of a theatrical center of first rank apparently due a city of this size has never been attained. The reasons for this were two-fold. In the early days of Newark there was a distinct survival of the New England puritanical dislike of the drama on wholly ethical grounds. When broader sympathies replaced this sentiment, the great theatrical center of the United States was fully established in New York City a short distance away and easy of access and consequently the theatre here had a competitor of the first rank at all times."

That theater in Newark had "more or less difficulty" has been chronicled on these pages. That theater entered the life of the city at all was due, perhaps, to what Matthew Arnold would call the "saving grace of a few." Great ages of theater, however, have never been maintained by the few. Theater is a group and public art. Newark, at the time that theater entered its life, was not a group; rather, it was several groups. Which of the groups would support a theater and for how long before their numbers had been exhausted? The answer to this appears time and again on these pages. The history of theater in Newark is also the history

121

of the cultural concerns of a city and of the persistence of various theater artists.

Why did the players come to Newark to begin with? and why did they continue to come? Many of them came in search of a theater of their own. The success of a short engagement encouraged them to invest further in the Newark Theatre. For other (particularly some of the stars) Newark simply offered another place to perform along the route of cities South and West. Many of the players found an audience in Newark, but none of them found an audience sufficiently large to support a continuing theatrical operation. Thus, the history of the theater in Newark is the record of sporadic efforts to establish a permanent stock company and of repeated return engagements of favorite players.

If Newark's proximity to New York hindered its independent cultural development, it also gave significance to those events which did take place. The history of the Newark Theater notes these varieties: stock players not associated at the time with a New York company, touring stars who did not include New York in their circuit, players whom New York later acclaimed as stars, and otherwise unrecorded performances of new plays. In addition, the history of the theater in Newark reflects, in abbreviated form, the American theater as exemplified in New York City.

Note on Appendices

On the pages that follow are listed 1) every play performed in Newark, 2) the dates of performance, 3) the place of performance, 4) every player who appeared, 5) the dates of his or her appearance, and 6) the play in which he or she appeared. There is, in addition, an indication of those performances which were presented as matinees as well as those presented for benefits.

Appendix A contains the list of plays. Appendix B contains the list of players. Both lists are alphabetically arranged. Each entry in both lists is followed by a year, month, and day or days of performance or appearance. All events should be assumed as having taken place at Concert Hall, the Newark Theatre, unless otherwise indicated. Other places of performance are indicated in Appendix A by the following abbreviations in parentheses following the day: (MH) Military Hall, (WH) Washington Hall, and (LH) Library Hall. Any other place of performance is written out and enclosed in parentheses, i. e. (Mansion House). In Appendix B the parentheses enclose numbers which indicate the play (as itemized in Appendix A) in which the particular player appeared on the given date. In both appendices a single asterisk (*) following a date indicates a matinee, a double asterisk (**) indicates both a matinee and evening performance of the play on that date.

Brackets are used in two ways in Appendix A. Variant

subtitles of a play are enclosed in brackets. Some dates of plays are enclosed in brackets. Dates so handled indicate amateur performances, prior to the construction of Concert Hall or during its first year of activity. In Appendix B a number symbol (#) following a date indicates a benefit performance for the particular player.

Since this study emerges in great part as a record of a single playhouse, Appendix A lists other performance items which appeared on the stage of Concert Hall. The reader will find, as a result, sixteen operas recorded, as well as pantomimes and ballets which were a part of the stock company's presentation. All of these departures are so indicated. In those instances in which only a scene or act of a play might be presented (as was often the case), the reader will find a note of this following the date.

Appendix A

List of Plays

1. Acting Mad. 1865: Jan 3, Jan 4, Jan 29.
2. Actress of all Work. 1849: Oct 11, Dec 23.
3. Adopted Child, The. 1847: May 21, May 25.
4. Advocate and the Orphan, The. 1865: Mar 25; 1867: Nov 14.
5. All Hallow Eve. 1867: Apr 10, Apr 11.
6. All Is a Farce. [1816: May 1].
7. All that Glitters Is Not Gold. 1865: Jan 26.
8. Alladin or The Wonderful Lamp. 1856: Jan 14, Jan 15, Jan 16, Jan 17, Jan 22, Jan 23, Jan 24.
9. Alladin or The Wonderful Scamp. 1867: Mar 29, Mar 30.
10. Allesandre Stradella, Opera of. 1856: Aug 18.
11. Alonzo the Brave. 1857: Mar 19.
12. Alpine Maid. 1853: Nov 21.
13. Ambrose Gwynette. 1848: May 6; 1852: Nov 18.
14. Ambition. 1861: Dec 18.
15. American Farmers, The or The Forest Rose. 1847: Je 4.
16. Anchor of Hope or The Tors of the Constition. 1852: Aug 7, Aug 9, (MH).
17. Andy Blake. 1867: Apr 22.
18. Angel and the Demon, The. 1865: Feb 17.
19. Angel of the Attic, The. 1847: May 27, Aug 2.
20. Animal Magnetism or True Science of Mesmerism. 1849: Dec 23.
21. Annexation of Cuba. 1852: Dec 11.
22. Antony and Cleopatra. 1867: May 9, May 11.
23. Apostate. 1852: Dec 1.
24. Archer of Switzerland. 1851: Mar 1. See also (?) 723 and 724.
25. Armadale. 1867: May 8, May 11.
26. Arrah Na Pogue or Wicklow Wedding. 1866: May 21, May 22.
27. Artemus Ward. 1867: Jan 2, Jan 3.
28. Artful Dodger, The. 1849: Dec 18; 1861: Oct 28; 1862: Mar 14, Mar 18.

29. As You Like It. 1850: Je 21 (Reading).
30. Asmaclius. 1856: Je 28.
31. Asmodeus. 1853: Jy 8 (MH).
32. Aurora Floyd or The Dark Deed in the Wood
    1865: Je 8.

33. Barber's Sport, The. 1863: Nov 16, Nov 17, Nov 18.
34. Barney, The Baron. 1861: Nov 16; 1862: Mar 24;
    1864: Dec 1; 1865: Mar 6, Mar 7; 1867: Oct 28,
    Oct 29.
35. Barnum Outdone. 1863: Mar 19, Mar 20, Apr 8 (LH).
36. Barnum Outwitted. 1856: JE 19.
37. Bashful Irishman, The. 1847: Je 29; 1849: Oct. 17.
38. Bath Road. 1847: Aug 20.
39. Bat's Vagaries or More Blunders Than One. 1857:
    Feb 5. See also 432.
40. Battle of Buena Vista. 1852: Nov 26, Nov 27, Dec 2.
41. Battle of Monterey, The. 1848: Jan 22, Jan 24.
42. Beauty and the Beast. 1867: Feb 25, Feb 26, Feb 27,
    Feb 28, Mar 1, Mar 2**.
43. Bel-Demonio. 1864: Dec 12, Dec 13, Dec 14.
44. Belle's Strategem. 1847: May 10; 1856: Je 28, Jy 1.
45. Ben Bolt. 1867: Mar 16.
46. Bertram. 1847: Aug 1, Aug 10, Aug 11.
47. Betsy Baker. 1865: Mar 9; 1867: Mar 5, Apr 18,
    May 14.
48. Black Blunder. 1861: Dec 11, Dec 12.
49. Black-Eyed Susan. 1847: Je 5, 1848: Apr 29, May 2;
    1849: Oct 25; 1852: Aug 2 (MH), Nov 3; 1856: Je 28;
    1857: Mar 7; 1860: Jan 2, May 25, May 26;
    1861: Dec 19; 1864: Sept 17, Nov 12; 1865: Feb 18,
    Mar 25, Jy 8; 1867: Jan 24, Jan 26, Oct 12,
    Nov 28*.
50. Blanche and Brandywine. 1861: Nov 27, Nov 28,
    Nov. 29.
51. Blind Boy. 1847: Jy 9.
52. Blondin on the Low Rope. 1864: Dec 26.
53. Bloomer Promenade, The. 1863: Nov 12, Nov 13.
54. Blue Devils. 1851: Feb 10, Feb 11; 1856: Jy 2, Jy 17.
55. Bluebeard. 1851: Jan 20, Jan 22, Jan 23, Jan 24.
56. Bob Nettles or A Schoolboy's Frolics. 1865: Jan 25.
57. Bohemian Girl, The, Opera of. 1860: Aug 23;
    1864: Apr 25, Apr 26, Apr 27, Apr 28 (LH).
58. Bombastes Furioso. 1863: May 13.
59. Born to Good Luck or The Irishman's Fortune. 1847:
    May 17, Je 28, Dec 23, Dec 25; 1849: Oct 4,
    Oct 18; 1867: Apr 5, Apr 6, May 1.

126

60. Bottle, The or The Drunkard's Dream or The
    Drunkard's Grave. 1847: Dec 25**, Dec 28,
    Dec 29.
61. Bowskin Gal, The or The Darkies Glory, Operatic
    Burlesque of. 1847: Oct 18, Oct 19, Oct 20.
62. Box and Cox. 1852: Oct 22 (MH); 1865: Mar 18 (LH).
63. Bride of Toulouse. 1853: Jy 29 (MH).
64. Brigand Queen or The Bandit of Abruzzi. 1865:
    Feb 27 (MH).
65. Brookwood. 1865: Feb 10.
66. Broom, The. 1852: Oct 18 (MH).
67. Brother Bill and Me. 1866. Dec 20.
68. Brother Bob and Me. 1867: Mar 27.
69. Browns, The. 1864: Nov 4.
70. Brutus or The Fall of Tarquins. 1848: May 16.
71. Brutus Locke Gears. 1859: Nov. 30.
72. Bryan O'Lynn. 1852: Oct 14 (MH); 1866: May 23.
73. Burlesque Circus. 1863: Feb 25, Feb 26 (LH).

74. Camille. 1857: Feb 19, Feb 20; 1862: Apr 28, Apr 29,
    Apr 30; [...or The Fate of a Coquette]. 1865:
    Jan 23, May 29; 1866: Nov 23.
75. Camille, Burlesque of. 1865: Jan 3, Jan 4.
76. Camille or The Cracked Heart. 1867: Jan 4.
77. Can a Woman Hold Her Tongue. 1865: Apr 12.
78. Captain Charlotte. 1867: Apr 17, Apr 18.
79. Captain Kyd. 1864: Nov 14, Nov 19.
80. Captain of the Watch, The. 1847: Je 16; 1850: Jy 10.
81. Captain's Not A-Miss. 1865: Apr 24.
82. Captive, The or A Tragic Scene in a Private Madhouse.
    1847: May 22, May 26, Aug 7.
83. Carnival of Venice. 1849: Nov 1.
84. Carpenter of Rouen. 1850: Nov 2; 1851: Feb 26; 1852:
    Nov 20; 1865: Apr 8.
85. Cataract of the Ganges, The. 1864: Sept 5, Sept 7;
    1865: May 29.
86. Catherine Hayes. 1852: Dec 18.
87. Cato's Soliloquy in Character. 1847: Dec 24.
88. Cattle Stealers, The or The Drover and His Dogs.
    1864: Jy 4.
89. Celestial Empire, The. 1852: Dec 7.
90. Chalk Line, The. 1850: Oct 5.
91. Challenge or The Yankee Will Fight. 1857: Mar 19.
92. Charles the Second or The Merry Monarch. 1847:
    May 4; 1852: Nov 16.

93. Charlotte Temple. 1861: Dec 3, Dec 6.
94. Cherry and Fair Star. 1865: Jan 31, Feb 1*, Feb 2*,
    Feb 3*, Feb 4**, Feb 6, Feb 7, Mar 27, Mar 28.
95. Chien et Chat. 1865: Mar 25 (Green Street Hall).
96. Child of the Regiment or Fortune of War. 1864: Dec
    30; 1867: Mar 25, Mar 30.
97. Children in the Wood. 1849: Dec 25*.
98. Cinderella. 1866: Dec 17, Dec 18.
99. Cinderella, Opera of. 1860: Aug 25; 1864: Apr 25,
    Apr 26, Apr 27, Apr 28 (LH).
100. Clandare, The Mountain Chieftain. 1856: Jan 8.
101. Classic Posturing. 1863: Apr 10.
102. Classical Grouping. 1863: Nov 12, Nov 13, Nov 14.
103. Cobbler and The Tailor, The. 1863: Nov 9, Nov 10,
    Nov 11.
104. Cobbler of Bagdad. 1848: Jan 27, Jan 28.
105. Cogger no Callie. 1866: May 17.
106. Colin or Nature and Philosophy. 1864: Oct 3; 1865:
    May 4. See also 454.
107. Colleen Bawn or The Brides of Garryowen. 1860: Jan
    5, May 25; 1861: Sept 2, Sept 3, Sept 5; 1864: Dec 5,
    Dec 6, Dec 7, Dec 10; 1865: Mar 10, Mar 11; 1866:
    Dec 3, Dec 4, Dec 5; 1867: Nov 6.
108. Comic Brothers, The. 1863: Nov 19.
109. Conjugal Lesson. 1864: Sept 24, Sept 26.
110. Connecticut Courtship. 1867: Apr 10, Apr 11.
111. Corsican Brothers, The or La Vendetta. 1860: Jan 4,
    Jan 5, May 25; 1861: Sept 10, Sept 11; 1864: Nov 17;
    1865: Feb 15, Mar 23, Mar 24; 1867: Mar 8, Mar 9,
    Nov 15.
112. Cousin Joe. 1852: Oct 6 (MH).
113. Cousin Joe's Visit. 1857: Nov 26*, Nov 27.
114. Crossing the Line. 1852: Oct 1, Oct 5 (MH); 1864:
    Nov 3, Dec 6; 1866: Dec 19.
115. Cudjo's Cave. 1864: Nov 21.
116. Cure, The. 1863: May 13.
117. Curfew, The. [1815: Dec 25; 1820: Apr 10, Apr 12.]
118. Customs of the Country. 1852: Oct 15 (MH); 1867:
    Apr 1, Apr 2, Apr 12.
119. Czar and Zimmerman or The Two Peters. 1859:
    Nov 15.

120. Damon and Pythias or The Test of Friendship. 1832:
    May 14 (Mansion House); 1847: Jy 29, Jy 30, Aug 4,
    Aug 21; 1848: May 25; 1852: Nov 8; 1856: May 12

(Mulberry Hall); 1857: Mar 10; 1860: Dec 19;
1861: Dec 24, Dec 26; 1862: May 5; 1867: Jan 26.
121. Dan, The Baron. 1867: May 4.
122. Daughter of the Regiment, Opera of. 1860: Aug 24;
1864: Apr 25, Apr 26, Apr 27, Apr 28 (LH).
123. Day After the Wedding, The or A Wife's First Lesson.
1832: May 15 (Mansion House); 1847: May 14, Je 1;
1848: May 26; 1852: Oct 20 (MH); 1867: Jan 31.   See
also 719.
124. Day in Paris, A. 1859: Mar 14; 1865: Apr 13.
125. Dead Shot, The. 1845: Je 25 (Show Boat); 1847: Jy 9,
Aug 23, Sept 6; 1848: May 23; 1849: Oct 5, Oct 23;
1854: Jan 26 (WH); 1864: Sept 22, Sept 27; 1865:
Jan 26; 1867: Dec 1.
126. Deaf Lover. 1849: Dec 19.
127. Dechalumeau. 1865: Apr 13.
128. Deeds of Dreadful Note. 1861: Nov 2.
129. Delicate Ground. 1853: Jy 28 (MH).
120. Der Freischeutz, Opera of. 1855: Je 2; 1859: Oct 20.
131. Devils Share, The. 1852: Dec 9.
132. Dick Turpin. 1864: Sept 2, Nov 24, Dec 25; 1865:
Jan 1, Jan 9, Feb 10, Mar 4, Mar 30.   See also
568.
133. Did You Ever Send Your Wife to New York?   1847:
Oct 4; 1849: Oct 8, Oct 24.
134. Doctor of Alcantare, Opera of.   1866: Oct 3, Oct 4,
Oct 5 (LH); 1867: Dec 2.
135. Dodging for a Wife.   1864: Feb 20 (Casino).
136. Dombey and Sons.   1857: Feb 6, Feb 18.
137. Don Caesar De Bazan.   1847: Je 30, Je 2; 1850: Oct 5;
1852: Oct 8 (MH), Nov 16; 1860: Jan 7; 1861: Sept
11, Dec 4; 1864: Nov 12, Nov 25; 1865: Feb 17,
Mar 24, Nov 15; 1867: Mar 7, Mar 29, Nov 15.
138. Douglass or The Noble Shepherd.   [1791: Sept 23];
[1815: Dec 11]; 1847: Jy 31; 1850: Jy 10; 1852:
Oct 19 (MH), Dec 22.
139. Dred of the Dismal Swamp.   1859: Feb 16.
140. Drunkard, The.   1850: Oct 26; 1852: Oct 6 (MH); 1856:
Mar 24, Mar 26 (WH); 1859: Apr 1; 1860: Nov 29**;
1861: Nov 27; 1862: Mar 12; 1864: Nov 15.
141. Drunkard and The Vagrant, The.   1850: Je 22.
142. Drunkard's Warning, The.   1846: Feb 27, Feb 28,
(Franklin Hall); 1849; Dec 17, Dec 18, Dec 19.
143. Drunkard's Wife, The.   1853: Aug 2 (MH).
144. Drunken Cobbler.   1832: May 17 (Mansion House).
145. Duchess of Malfi.   1867: Oct 1, Oct 2.

146. Dumb Belle, The. 1847: Apr 17, Je 4, Apr 14, Aug
     14; 1852: Oct 23 (MH); 1853: Nov 2; 1857: Mar 11,
     Mar 12; 1864: Oct 3.
147. Dumb Boy of Manchester, The. 1867: Nov 21.
148. Dumb Girl of Genoa, The or The Bandit Merchant.
     1847: Je 24; 1849: Dec 19.
149. Dumb Waiter, The. 1860: Dec 24, Dec 25*.

150. East Lynne [...or The Earl's Daughter]. 1865: Jan 16,
     Jan 17; 1866: Je 11, Je 12; [...or Elopement].
     1867: Feb 1, Mar 14, Oct 11.
151. Eaton Boy. 1851: Feb 15; 1852: Oct 21 (MH); 1864:
     Sept 9.
152. Eccentric Lover. 1849: Dec 25*. See also 532.
153. Elizabeth--Queen of England. 1867: Nov 25.
154. Elves, The or The Statue Bride. 1866: Dec 21.
155. Emerald Island, The or Ireland As It Is. 1847: Jy 3.
     See also 268 and 269.
156. Ernestine or Which Is My Cousin? 1847: May 25, May
     28.
157. Esmeralda. 1852: Nov 3.
158. Essence of Old Virginny (Old Mac). 1867: May 2,
     May 3.
159. Eustache, The Man of the Mountain. 1867: Jan 30.
160. Eustache Baudin or Love and Bride. 1861: Dec 2;
     1864: Nov 2, Nov 3; 1865: Jan 19.
161. Eva, The Irish Princess. 1867: Nov 1, Nov 5.
162. Evadne or The Statue. 1852: Oct 25 (MH).
163. Exempt Brigade. 1863: Apr 10.

164. Factory Girl. 1861: Sept 6.
165. Faint Heart Never Won Fair Lady. 1847: May 14, Jy 31;
     1850: Jy 15; 1852: Sept 24 (MH); 1853: Nov 2; 1861:
     Dec 3; 1864: Nov 22; 1865: Jan 21; 1867: Nov 14.
166. Fairy Islands, The. 1865: Apr 5.
167. Fallen Saved, The. 1867: Mar 1, Mar 2.
168. Family Circle, The. 1867: Apr 1, Apr 2.
169. Family Jars. 1847: Aug 10; 1851: Feb 5; 1865: Mar
     29; 1867: Apr 17, Apr 20.
170. Fanchon, the Cricket. 1864: Nov 7, Nov 8, Nov 9;
     1865: May 2; 1867: Apr 23, Oct 10.
171. Fashion or Life in the City. 1867: Jan 24.
172. Fashion and Famine. 1855: Nov 10.
173. Fate or Children of Love. 1857: Mar 2, Mar 3.

174. Father Kemp's Old Folks. 1862: Mar 21, Mar 22.
175. Favorite Afterpiece. 1857: Mar 5.
176. Favorite Piece, A. 1851: Feb 13.
177. Fazio or The Italian Wife. 1847: May 11, May 14, May 15, Aug 16; 1848: Apr 29; 1852: Dec 13.
178. Female American Spy, The or Scenes in the Great Rebellion. 1865: Mar 31.
179. Female Detective, The. 1867: Apr 19, Apr 20.
180. Female Horse Thief, The. 1864: Sept. 6.
181. Female Husband, The. 1850: Aug 17.
182. Fencing Matches. 1847: Jy 2, Jy 5.
183. Fete of Shakespeare, The. 1852: Oct 18 (MH).
184. Fire Raisers, The. 1851: Jan 25.
185. Fireman. 1862: May 3.
186. Flower of Erin. 1865: Jy 6.
187. Flower of the Flock, The. 1863: Feb 25, Feb 26 (LH).
188. Flowers of the Forest. 1867: Mar 4.
189. Flying Dutchman, The. 1866: Dec 24, Dec 25, Dec 26, Dec 27.
190. Follies of the Night 1856: Je 24.
191. Fool of the Family. 1866: Dec 21.
192. Foreign Prince or Jim Crow in London. 1847: Apr 17; 1849: Oct 27, Nov 1; 1852: Oct 2, Oct 4 (MH).
193. Forest Princess, The or Two Centuries Ago. 1848: May 1, May 2..
194. Forest Rose. 1852: Dec 18; 1857: Mar 18; 1862: May 17.
195. Forged Will. 1857: Mar 17.
196. Fortune's Frolic [...or Clown Turned Lord]. 1832: May 9 (Mansion House); [...or Ploughman Turned Lord]. 1848: May 19; 1860: May 26.
197. Fortune's Whim. 1852: Oct 15 (MH).
198. Forty Thieves, The. 1849: Dec 25; 1850: Je 22; 1865: Apr 1; 1866: Dec 31.
199. Forty Winks. 1867: Jan 18, Jan 19.
200. Foundling, The or The Wild Horse of the Prairie. 1865: Jy 21.
201. Four Sisters. 1860: May 23; 1865: Jan 24, Jan 25; 1867: Nov 20, Nov 22.
202. Fra Diavalo, Opera of. 1866: Dec 20.
203. Fratricide, The. 1852: Dec 17.
204. French Spy, The or The Fall of Algiers. 1852: Nov 5; 1856: Jy 10; 1859: Mar 14; 1864: Aug 31, Sept 1, Sept 29, Nov 25, Dec 24, Dec 25; 1865: Jan 10, Feb 24, Feb 25, Mar 1; 1866: Jan 22; 1867: Mar 5, Mar 6, Mar 7, Nov 18, Nov 19, Nov 23.

205. Frightened Servant, The. 1857: Mar 21.
206. Frisky Cobbler, The. 1863: Apr 28.
207. Frolics of Love, The. 1864: Jan 2.

208. Gamester. 1853: Oct 28.
209. George. 1861: Dec 11, Dec 12.
210. George Barnwell or The London Apprentice. 1799:
     Aug 21 (Newark Academy); 1857: Feb 21; 1861:
     Nov 16.
211. Ghost, The. 1864: Sept 10; 1865: Jan 26, May 6.
212. Gibble Gobble Family, The. 1863: Apr 6.
213. Gipsey's Warning, The. 1857: Nov 26.
214. Glance at New York in 1848, A. 1848: May 26;
     1849: Oct 9, Oct 16, Oct 17, Oct 24.
215. Gold vs. Greenbacks. 1863: Apr 6.
216. Golden Farmer. 1852: Oct 9 (MH); 1867: Jan 5;
     [...or The Last Crime]. 1847: Je 19, Je 22.
217. Golden Farmer, The or Vell Vot of It. 1847: Dec 29.
218. Good for Nothing, The. 1860: Mar 17; 1864: Aug 31;
     [or Good for Nothing, That]. 1857: Nov 23, Nov 26.
     See also 449.
219. Good Night's Rest, A. 1847: Dec 23.
220. Governor's Wife. 1852: Nov 29; 1867: Apr 22.
221. Graceful Groupings. 1865: Apr 13.
222. Grandfather Whitehead. 1847: Je 4.
223. Great Attraction. 1854: Jan 30 (WH).
224. Green Bushel. 1865: Jan 1.
225. Green Bushes [...or Huntress of the Missippi].
     1867: Mar 18, Mar 19, Mar 20, Mar 21, Mar 22;
     [...or One-Hundred Years Ago]. 1864: Sept 26;
     1865: Mar 13.
226. Griffith Gaunt or Jealousy. 1867: Feb 18, Feb 19,
     Feb 20, Feb 21, May 6, May 7.
227. Gun-Maker of Moscow. 1867: Jan 9.
228. Guy Mannering or The Gipsey's Prophecy. 1866: Nov
     19, Nov 20, Nov 21, Nov 22; 1867: Feb 11, Feb 12,
     Apr 25, Oct 3.

229. Hamlet. 1847: Je 1, Aug 12; 1848: May 22; 1849:
     Nov 13 (LH); 1851: Feb 4; 1853: Nov 3 (Scenes
     from); 1857: Feb 17, Nov 24; 1860: Jan 3, May 22
     (LH) (Reading), May 24; 1861: Sept 9, Nov 15; 1864:
     Dec 20; 1865: Feb 16, Mar 20, Nov 6, Nov 7, Nov
     8, Nov 9, Nov 10, Nov 11; 1866: Dec 6; 1867: Jan
     22, Nov 11.

230. Hamlet or The Wearing of the Black. 1867: Jan 2, Jan 3.
231. Handy Andy. 1865: Jan 3, Jan 4, Apr 24; 1867: Apr 29, Apr 30.
232. Happy Man, The or The Magic Shirt. 1847: Je 16, Je 19; 1849: Oct 5, Oct 8; Apr 5, Apr 6. See also 390.
233. Harrold Hawk. 1861: Aug 31.
234. Harry Burnham. 1853: Jy 30 (MH).
235. Hatter and The Printer, The. 1852: Oct 11 (MH).
236. Haymakers. 1860: Feb 7.
237. Hazardous Ground. 1867: Feb 22, Feb 23.
238. Hecate. 1853: Nov 21.
239. Here She Goes, and There She Goes. 1863: Nov 12, Nov 13.
240. Hidden Hand, The. 1861: Nov 7, Nov 11, Nov 12, Nov 13, Nov 14; 1862: Mar 24, Mar 29; 1865: Mar 14; 1867: Jan 12.
241. His Last Legs. 1847: Je 11; 1851: Oct 1; 1854: Jan 31 (WH); 1858: Jy 3; 1861: Nov 1; 1864: Dec 2; 1867: May 3, May 4.
242. His Last Victory. 1865: Je 9.
243. Hole in the Wall. 1864: Nov 17; 1865: Jan 20. See also 594 and 646.
244. Home Again. 1861: Nov 27.
245. Honeymoon, The or How to Rule a Wife. 1847: Apr 9, May 13, May 22, Aug 7; 1849: Oct 11; 1852: Nov 2; 1861: Dec 24, Dec 26; 1862: May 3; 1866: Nov 15; 1867: Dec 1.
246. Hot Corn. 1855: Nov 13.
247. Hotel D'Afrique. 1855: May 9.
248. Hour in Ireland, An. 1857: Feb. 6.
249. How to Become an Actor. 1863: Nov 6.
250. How to Cheat a Man. 1848: Oct 26.
251. How to Pay the Rent. 1847: May 11, May 14, Je 17.
252. Humors of Splash. 1849: Dec 23.
253. Hunchback. 1847: May 8, May 12; 1848: May 10; 1849: Oct 12; 1850: Je 4; 1853: Oct 25; 1866: Nov 13; 1867: May 20, Sept 30.
254. Hunchback of Notre Dame or Quasimodo. 1867: Apr 13.
255. Hunting a Turtle. 1847: Apr 10.
256. Husband at Sight. 1860: May 23; 1865: May 6.

257. I Know a Bank. 1847: Dec 24.

258. Idiot Witness. 1852: Aug 10 (MH); 1861: Sept 7; 1866: Nov 24; [...or Murder of the Heath]. 1848: May 25; [... or Queen's Page]. 1847: Je 21; [...or The Solitary of the Heath]. 1847: Dec. 22.
259. Il Travatore, Opera of. 1856: Jy 29; 1860: Aug 21.
260. Il Travatore, Burlesque of. 1859: Je 20.
261. In and Out of Place. 1865: Apr 21; 1867: Apr 3, Apr 4.
262. Ingamar, The Barbarian. 1854: Jan 14, Jan 15, Jan 16; 1857: Feb 5; 1867: Mar 13.
263. Inkeeper of Abbeville, The. 1852: Aug 14 (MH).
264. Inshavogue or Outlaw of '98, The. 1867: Oct 28.
265. Invisible Prince, The. 1866: Dec 22.
266. Invisible Queen, The. 1866: Dec 19.
267. Ireland and America. 1864: Dec 8.
268. Ireland As It Is. 1852: Oct 12, Oct 14, Oct 16 (MH); 1864: Sept 15; 1865: Jan 12; 1866: May 19. See also 269 and 155.
269. Ireland As It Was. 1860: Mar 22, Mar 24; 1865: Feb 25, Mar 3; 1867: Apr 3, Apr 4, Oct 29. See also 268 and 155.
270. Irish Assurance and Yankee Modesty. 1861: Dec 21; 1864: Dec 9, Dec 10; 1865: Mar 8, Mar 9, Apr 24.
271. Irish Dragoon or Wards in Chancery. 1847: Je 24.
272. Irish Emigrant, The. 1861: Dec 25; 1862: Mar 17, Mar 22; 1865: Jan 5. See also 642.
273. Irish Engagement, An. 1849: Oct 19.
274. Irish Heiress, The. 1853: Aug 1 (MH).
275. Irish Lilt. 1852: Aug 20 (MH).
276. Irish Lion, The. 1847: Je 8, Jy 1, Oct 7; 1849: Oct 3, Oct 5, Oct 9, Dec 20; 1851: Feb 4; 1852: Oct 8 (MH); 1853: Oct 29; 1858: Jy 17; 1862: Mar 27; 1865: Apr 21; 1867: Apr 12, May 2.
277. Irish Post. 1847: Jy 3.
278. Irish Tiger, The. 1860: Mar 22, Mar 23; 1865: Apr 22; 1867: Apr 12.
279. Irish Tutor or New Lights. 1847: Apr 9, Dec 22; 1849: Oct 4, Oct 16; 1852: Oct 21, Oct 22, (MH); 1854: Jan 27 (WH); 1866: Dec 19; 1867: Nov 1, Nov 5. See also 460.
280. Iron Chest or Mysterious Murderer, The. 1832: May 15, (Mansion House).
281. Iron Chest, The or Force of Conscience. 1847: Aug 6.
282. Iron Mask, The. 1860: May 26.
283. Is He Jealous. 1847: Aug 9, Aug 25.
284. I've Eaten My Friend. 1852: Aug 10, Aug 11, (MH).

285. Jack Cabbage Among the Nobs. 1864: Dec 30.
286. Jack Cade or Bondsmen of Kent. 1860: Jan 6;
     1861: Oct 30; 1865: Feb 14, Nov 14; 1867: May 13,
     May 16, Nov 12.
287. Jack Humphries. 1856: Je 30.
288. Jack Sheppard. 1852: Aug 16 (MH), Nov 5; 1856:
     Jy 9; 1861: Nov 9, Nov 16; 1862: Mar 28; 1864:
     Sept 7, Oct 1, Nov 19, Dec 17; 1865: Feb 11,
     Feb 25, Mar 18; 1867: Jan 5.
289. Jack's The Lad. 1852: Aug 13, Aug 14 (MH).
290. Jacobite, The. 1853: Nov 2.
291. Jane Shore or The Unhappy Favorite. 1854: Jan 12.
292. Jealous Wife. 1856: Jy 14. See also 595.
293. Jeanette and Jeannot. 1863: Nov 6.
294. Jeem's, The Poet. 1863: Apr 10.
295. Jenny Foster. 1865: Je 9.
296. Jenny Lind. 1856: Je 24; 1866: Nov 12, Nov 15; 1867:
     Mar 15.
297. Jenny Lind, Opera of. 1862: Mar 26, Mar 29; 1865:
     Feb 24, Feb 27.
298. Jeremiah Clip. 1847: Aug 12. See also 714.
299. Jersey Blue, A. 1847: Je 26.
300. Jesse Brown or The Relief of Lucknow. 1865: Jan 27,
     Jan 28.
301. Jewess or The Council of Constance. 1854: Jan 21.
302. Jim Crow at Court. 1849: Oct 29.
303. Joan of Arc. 1866: Nov 17.
304. Jobin et Nanette. 1865: Mar 25 (Green Street Hall).
305. Jocko, The Brazilian Ape. 1865: Apr 5, Apr 11.
306. John Bull. [1816: May 1].
307. John Bull in France. 1850: Oct 26.
308. John Doolittle's Courtship. 1863: Mar 19.
309. John Jones or I'm Hunted by a Friend. 1847: May 26.
310. John Jones of the War Office. 1861: Nov 25, Nov 26.
311. John Wopps. 1867: Jan 2, Jan 3.
312. Jolly Cobbler. 1851: May 17.
313. Jonathan in England. 1847: Je 7.
314. Jonathan Slick. 1845: May 8 (MH).
315. Jones' Baby. 1866: Dec 7, Dec 11.
316. Joseph and His Brethren. 1862: Mar 27.
317. Julius Caesar. 1847: Dec 24, (Act 3); 1865: Nov 17;
     1867: Nov 13.
318. Jumbo Jim. 1847: Apr 15; 1849: Oct 26, Oct 27, Oct
     31; 1852: Sept 29, Sept 30, Oct 23 (MH).

319. Karmel, The Scot or The Rebels or the Jerseys.
        1857: Mar 12, Mar 13, Mar 14.
320. Kate Kearny. 1849: Oct 9, Oct 16.
321. Katharine and Petruchio. 1847: May 28, May 31;
        1852: Oct 21 (MH); 1857: Mar 13; 1867: Feb 2.
322. Kathleen Mavourneen. 1867: Nov 8, Nov 9.
323. Kenilworth. 1867: Mar 26, Mar 27, Mar 28.
324. Kill or Cure. 1847: Je 23.
325. King Lear. 1847: Aug 20; 1853: Nov 2 (Scenes from).
326. King Lear, The Cuss. 1866: Dec 31.
327. Kiss in the Dark. 1853: Aug 1 (MH); 1854: Jan 31
        (WH); 1856: Jy 17; 1862: Mar 12; 1865: Feb 21;
        1866: Dec 21; 1867: Apr 26, May 8.
328. Knight and the Cobbler, The. 1852: Nov 27.
329. Knight of Arva, The. 1866: Nov 30.

330. La Costeminetak. 1863: Nov 21.
331. La Meuniere de Marly. 1865: Mar 21 (Green Street
        Hall).
332. La Peche Equepoise. 1863: Apr 21, Apr 23, Nov 9,
        Nov 10, Nov 11.
333. La Polka. 1847: Dec 25*.
334. La Statue Blanche. 1863: May 13, Oct 5 (Pantomime),
        Oct 6 (Pantomime).
335. La Tour de Nesle or The Chamber of Death. 1848:
        May 4; 1849: Oct 15; 1851: Jan 28; 1852: Oct 1 (MH);
        1853: Nov 3; 1861: Oct 31; 1864: Sept 30; 1867:
        Nov 30.
336. Ladies' Battle or Duel of Love. 1864: Feb 10 (LH).
337. Lady and The Devil. 1847: Je 3.
338. Lady Audley's Secret or The Mystery of Audley Court.
        1867: Mar 11, Mar 12, Mar 15.
339. Lady of Lyons, The. 1847: Apr 15, May 7, May 13,
        May 26, Je 25, Jy 1, Oct 4; 1848: Apr 27; 1850:
        Oct 7; 1851: Jan 18, Feb 5, Dec 16; 1852: Aug 20,
        Sept 24, (MH); 1853: Jy 2 (MH), Oct 27; 1860:
        Dec 20; 1861: Dec 5; 1865: Jan 13, Jan 24; 1866:
        Nov 14; 1867: May 9.
340. Lady of the Lake. 1849: Nov 3.
341. Last Days of Pompeii, The. 1857: Nov 28; 1861:
        Nov. 1.
342. Last Legs. 1852: Oct 20 (MH).
343. Le Chalet, Opera of. 1847: Je 25, Je 28.
344. Le Maitre Francais. 1863: Mar 26.

345. Le Mari de la Dame de Chocures. 1865: Mar 21
     (Green Street Hall).
346. Leah, The Forsaken. 1867: Mar 16.
347. L'Echelle Perileuse. 1863: Nov 19.
348. Lend Me Five Shillings. 1854: Jan 21.
349. Les Aanslurs de Mal. 1863: Nov 26, Nov 27.
350. Les Deux Divorces. 1865: Mar 25 (Green Street
     Hall).
351. Lesson for Husbands, A. 1864: Nov 28.
352. Lightwood and Thunderbolt. 1864: Sept 3.
353. Like Master Like Man. 1852: Nov 30.
354. Lime Kiln Man. 1865: Jan 20, Jan 21.
355. Limerick Boy. 1847: Jy 2; 1849: Oct 3, Oct 6, Oct 12;
     1852: Oct 2, Oct 15, Oct 16 (MH), Nov 29, Dec
     24 (MH); 1853: Aug 1 (MH).
356. Lioness of the North. 1867: May 10.
357. Little Devil, The or My Slave. 1865: Mar 3.
358. Live Indian. 1867: Jan 15, Jan 16.
359. Lively Barrel, The. 1863: Nov 12, Nov 13, Nov 14.
360. Loan of a Lover. 1845: Je 23 (Show Boat); 1847:
     Je 5; 1852: Nov 12; 1854: Jan 30 (WH); 1865: Feb
     20, Mar 2.
361. Locomotive Explosion, A. 1863: Nov 26, Nov 28.
362. Lola Montez. 1851: Feb 24, Feb 25; 1852: Aug 13
     (MH), Nov 9, Nov 10, Nov 11; 1853: Aug 2 (MH);
     1866: Dec 20.
363. Lollipop Lumkins. 1861: Dec 6.
364. London Assurance. 1852: Sept 25, Oct 7 (MH); 1855:
     Je 18, Je 19, Je 20; 1866: Nov 8, Nov 9, Nov 10.
365. Long Strike, The. 1867: Oct 30, Oct 31, Nov 2.
366. Lord Barney. 1864: Dec 8; 1866: May 17.
367. Lottery Ticket, The or The Hunchback Clerk. 1848:
     May 9, May 18, May 20, May 26; 1849: Nov 29;
     1852: Aug 16, Aug 21 (MH).
368. Love or The Countess and the Serf. 1847: Aug 2.
369. Love and Medicine. 1864: Aug 26.
370. Love and Murder. 1867: Oct 30, Oct 31.
371. Love Chase. 1854: Jan 10; 1855: Dec 14; 1857: Feb 19,
     Feb 20.
372. Love in All Corners. 1864: Sept 24.
373. Love in Humble Life. 1847: Dec 28.
374. Love of Longitude, The. 1865: Apr 13.
375. Love Under the Door, The. 1848: Oct 25.
376. Love's Sacrifice or The Rival Merchants. 1847: Sept
     3, Oct 7; 1848: Apr 28; 1852: Nov 12; 1857: Nov 27.

377. Lucia di Lammermoor, Opera of. 1861: Nov 2, Nov 4 (LH) (Last Act).
378. Lucille or The Story of the Heart or Love, Ambition, and Retribution. 1850: Jy 15.
379. Lucinda at the Soiree. 1863: Mar 19.
380. Lucretia Borgia, Opera of. 1854: Jan 11, Jan 13; 1855: Dec 14; 1856: Jy 28; 1860: Aug 22, Dec 22; 1861: Nov 2, Nov 4; 1864: Sept 22; 1866: Nov 24.
381. Lucy Long. 1849: Dec 25, (WH).
382. Lumpacuvagabusdus. 1851: May 14.
383. Lying Valet. 1854: Feb 1 (WH).
384. Lysiah, The Abandoned. 1865: Feb 21.

385. Macbeth. 1847: Aug 23, Aug 25, Sept 6; 1848: May 18, May 19, May 20; 1849: Nov 5 (LH) (Dagger Scene); 1853: Oct 31 (Readings from), Nov 21; 1857: Nov 25; 1861: Dec 16; 1864: Dec 19; 1865: Feb 13, Mar 21, Nov 16; 1866: Dec 8*, Dec 12; 1867: Apr 27, Sept. 28.
386. Maccasophos. [1791: Je (?) and Jy 4].
387. Madelaine or The Founding of Farbourg. 1852: Dec 20, Dec 21; 1867: Oct 12.
388. Magic Box, The. 1863: Nov 27, Nov 28, Nov 30.
389. Magic Flute, The. 1863: Apr 24.
390. Magic Shirt. 1852: Dec 16. See also 232.
391. Magic Trumpet, The. 1865: Apr 3, Apr 7.
392. Maid of Munster or Cork Leg. 1848: May 13; 1861: Dec 7; 1864: Dec 8; 1865: Jan 13. See also 508.
393. Maid of Saragossa. 1852: Nov 9, Nov 10, Nov 11.
394. Make Your Wills. 1852: Nov 24, Dec 2, Dec 18.
395. Malvisi. 1851: Oct 1.
396. Man. 1865: May 5.
397. Man of Fortitude, The or The Nice Adventure. 1827: Mar 17, Mar 18, Mar 19, Mar 20, Mar 21, Mar 22 (Morton's Concert Room).
398. Maniac. 1856: Jy 7.
399. Maniac Lover, The. 1861: Oct 31. See also 415.
400. Marble Head or The Sculptor's Dream. 1866: Feb 22*.
401. Marble Heart. 1864. Sept. 27
402. Marco, The Mute. 1867: Nov 22.
403. Market Girl, The. 1865: May 3.
404. Married Blind. 1857: Mar 17, Mar 18.
405. Married Life. 1852: Nov 18; 1866: Dec 7; 1867: Jan 14, Nov 28.

138

406. Married Rake, The. 1847: Jy 29; 1852: Oct 7 (MH);
     1854: Jan 13, Jan 17; 1860: May 26.
407. Martha or The Fair of Richmond, Opera of. 1856:
     Aug 5.
408. Mary Stuart. 1851: Dec 15; 1867: Dec 3.
409. Masks and Faces. 1864: Oct 3.
410. Matteo Falcone or The Brigand and His Son. 1847:
     Jy 8; 1849: Dec 7; 1851: Mar 1; 1852: Aug 2 (MH).
411. Mazeppa or The Untamed Rocking Horse. 1865: Jan 6,
     Jan 7; 1866: Dec 24, Dec 25, Dec 26, Dec 27.
412. Mazeppa or The Wild Horse of Tartary. 1851: Feb 10,
     Feb 11; 1862: Apr 21; 1864: Aug 24, Aug 25, Aug
     26, Sept 2, Nov 24, Nov 26, Dec 15, Dec 25;
     1865: Jy 19; 1866: May 29.
413. Merchant of Venice. 1847: May 18, Jy 3; 1848:
     May 24; 1852: Aug 16, Sept 27 (MH) (Act 4);
     1858: Jy 3.
414. Merry Cobbler, The. 1861: Dec 16.
415. Michael Erle. 1860: Mar 24; 1866: Nov 17; 1867:
     Mar 9, May 4, Nov 30. See also 399.
416. Middy Ashore. 1852: Aug 4, Aug 6, Sept 28, Sept
     29, Oct 13, Oct 25 (MH); 1853: Jy 29 (MH);
     1856: Jan 23.
417. Midnight Attack, The. 1865: Apr 11.
418. Mike Martin, The Bold Irish Robber and Highwayman.
     1851: Feb 12, Feb 13.
419. Milea's Boy. 1856: Jy 8.
420. Miller of New Jersey, The. 1859: Dec 30.
421. Mischievous Monkey. 1863: Feb 25, Feb 26, Apr
     3 (LH).
422. Mischievous Negro, The. 1861: Dec 5.
423. Miser of South Wales. 1852: Nov 25.
424. Miseries of New York, The. 1849: Oct 25.
425. Mock Doctor, The or The Dumb Lady Cured. 1799:
     Aug 7.
426. Model of a Wife. 1849: Oct 25; 1850: Oct 7; 1852:
     Nov 17; 1856: Jy 12.
427. Moll Pitcher or The Witch of Lynn. 1857: Mar 20,
     Mar 21; 1866: May 19, May 23.
428. Money. 1851: Feb 17; 1862: Dec 3 (LH).
429. Monsieur Guguignon. 1865: Apr (?).
430. Monsieur Jacques. 1847: May 5.
431. Monsieur Mallet or The Post Office Mistake. 1847:
     Jy 7.
432. More Blunders Than One. 1865: Jan 5, Jan 7; 1867:
     May 1, May 2. See also 39.

139

433. Mose in California. 1849: Oct 22, Oct 23; 1851: May 31, Je 2.
434. Mose in San Francisco. 1849: Oct 18, Oct 19, Oct 20.
435. Mother and Child Are Doing Fine. 1855: Nov 19, Nov 20.
436. Mountain Archer. 1861: Dec 13.
437. Mountain Outlaw. 1865: Jan 16.
438. Mr. Heal Erle. 1853: Oct 29.
439. Mr. Thrale's Three Warnings or Death--An Unwelcome Visitor. 1799: Aug 7.
440. Mr. and Mrs. Peter White. 1851: Feb 14; 1852: Aug 5 (MH); 1853: Oct 27; 1864: Nov 2, Dec 7; 1867: Feb 25, Feb 26, Feb 27, Feb 28.
441. Mrs. Wiggins. [1820: Apr 10, Apr 12].
442. Mummy, The. 1851: Feb 27; 1852: Sept 29, Sept 30 (MH), Nov 8.
443. Murder of the Roadside. 1852: Nov 24.
444. My Aunt. 1847: May 18, May 20.
445. My Neighbor's Wife. 1864: Feb 10 (LH).
446. My Wife's Mirror. 1861: Nov 15.
447. Mysterious Stranger, The. 1865: Apr 10*; 1867: Jan 31. See also 587.

448. Nabob for an Hour, A. 1851: Jan 18. See also 677.
449. Nan, The Good for Nothing. 1861: Mar 15; 1865: Feb 9; 1866: Dec 17, Dec 18; 1867: Apr 16, Apr 18. See also 218.
450. Naomi, The Deserted. 1866: Dec 10, Dec 11.
451. Napoleon's Old Guard. 1847: May 12, May 17, Je 18, Jy 6; 1852: Sept 27 (MH).
452. Narmatta or The Wept of Wish-Tom-Wish. 1865: Feb 23. See also 708.
453. Nature and Art. 1863: Feb 28 (LH).
454. Nature and Philosophy. 1852: Aug 10, Aug 21, Sept 27, Sept 28, Oct 19 (MH); 1864: Sept 6; 1865: Jan 12, Feb 8. See also 106.
455. Naval Engagements. 1851: Feb 19, Feb 21; 1866: Jy 4**.
456. Nettles. 1856: Jy 9.
457. Never Too Late to Mend. 1866: May 14.
458. New Jersey First, The or Scenes on the Potomac. 1862: Mar 28.
459. New Jersey in 1776. 1860: Dec 25.
460. New Lights. 1847: Je 30. See also 279.

461. New Notions. 1853: Oct 25.
462. New Year Calls. 1860: Jan 9, Jan 10.
463. New York As It Is. 1856: Jy 12.
464. Newark Firemen. 1852: Dec 4, Dec 6, Dec 7,
     Dec 8, Dec 9, Dec 10, Dec 11, Dec 13, Dec 14,
     Dec 15, Dec 16; 1861: Nov 30.
465. Newark Mechanic. 1857: Mar 20.
466. Newark Workman. 1865: Apr 25, Apr 26, Apr 27,
     Apr 28.
467. Nick of the Woods. 1850: Nov 2; 1851: Feb 20;
     1856: Jan 8; 1857: Mar 9, Mar 11; 1860: Jan 7;
     1861: Dec 9, Dec 10; 1864: Sept 29, Dec 24;
     1865: Apr 29; 1867: May 14, May 17, May 18.
468. Nine Points of the Law. 1867: Mar 28.
469. No Song No Supper or The Lawyer in the Sack. 1799:
     Aug 7; 1832: May 14 (Mansion House).
470. Nobody's Daughter. 1867: Oct 7, Oct 8, Oct 9.
471. Norah Creina. 1865: Jan 14, Jan 17.
472. Norma, Opera of. 1863: Feb 5 (LH).

473. Object of Interest, An. 1865: Feb 27; 1867: Mar 13,
     Mar 14, Apr 19, May 15.
474. Octavia Brigaldi or The Confession. 1849: Oct 15.
475. Octoroon, The or Life in Louisiana. 1861: Nov 4,
     Nov 5, Nov 6, Nov 7, Nov 8, Nov 9, Nov 14;
     1865: Mar 11; 1867: Feb 4, Feb 5, Feb 6, Feb 7,
     Feb 8, Feb 9, Feb 15, Feb 16, Feb 22*. See
     also 754.
476. O'Flannigan and The Fairies. 1867: Nov 2, Nov 6.
477. Oh! Hush! 1863: Apr 16.
478. Old and Young or The Four Monkeys. 1847: Dec 22,
     Dec 24; 1859: Nov 24**, Nov 26**.
479. Old Guard. 1854: Jan 30 (WH).
480. Oliver Twist. 1860: Jan 2; 1864: Dec 15; 1867:
     Oct 25, Oct 26.
481. Omnibus, The or A Convenient Distance. 1847:
     Je 18, Jy 10; 1849: Oct 6, Oct 17, Oct 22;
     1852: Oct 20 (MH); 1853: Jy 28 (MH).
482. One, Two, Three, Four, Five. 1856: Jy 8.
483. Orion, The Gold Beater or True Hearts and False.
     1857: Mar 4, Mar 5, Mar 7.
484. Orphans of Geneva. 1861: Dec 7. See also 648.
485. Otello, Moor of Orange Street. 1849: Oct 29, Oct 30,
     Oct 31.

141

486. Othello.   1832: May 19 (Mansion House); 1847: Apr 13,
     Apr 16, Apr 17 (Burlesque of), May 19; 1848: May
     11, May 15; 1851: Jan 29; 1852: Oct 2, Oct 4, Oct
     5 (MH) (Burlesque of); 1858: Jy 31; 1860: May 25
     (LH) (Reading); 1861: Oct 29; 1862: May 2; 1864:
     Dec 22; 1866: Dec 13; 1867: Apr 26.
487. Our African Cousin.   1849: Oct 20.
488. Our American Cousin.   1862: Mar 25, Mar 26;
     1865: Apr 12; 1867: Jan 4.
489. Our Country Cousin.   1866: Dec 22.
490. Our Female American Cousin.   1859: Mar 5.
491. Our Gal.   1852: Oct 12, Oct 16 (MH); 1860:   Mar 23;
     1865: Apr 22.
492. Our Mutual Friend.   1867: Jan 28, Jan 29.
493. Out on a Spree.   1865: Apr 12.
494. Outahlanchet or The Lion of the Forest.   1861: Dec
     14, Dec 17; 1867: May 15.
495. Oxford Student, The.   1827: Mar 17, Mar 18, Mar 19,
     Mar 20, Mar 21, Mar 22 (Morton's Concert Room).

496. Paddy, The Piper.   1853: Aug 1 (MH); 1864: Dec 3.
497. Paddy Miles.   1852: Dec 23, Dec 24; 1861: Dec 25*;
     1865: Apr 22.
498. Paddy Miles' Boy.   1849: Oct 18; 1861: Sept 2, Sept 3,
     Dec 18; 1865: Mar 2.
499. Paddy's Trip to America.   1849: Oct 20.
500. Patience and Perserverance.   1867: Apr 8, Apr 9.
501. Patriot's Dream.   1861: Nov 20, Nov 21, Nov 22,
     Nov 23.
502. Paul Jones.   1851: Feb 26; 1865: Je 10.
503. Paul Pry.   1856: Jy 11, Jy 15; 1867: Jan 16.
504. Pay Too Late.   1865: May 1, May 6.
505. Peep O'Day or Savoureen Relish.   1864: Nov 28, Dec 1,
     Dec 2, Dec 3; 1865: Mar 6, Mar 7; 1867: Nov 4,
     Nov 7.
506. Peggy Green.   1867: Mar 26.
507. People's Lawyer, The.   1856: Jy 10; 1857: Mar 6;
     1864: Nov 18.
508. Perfection or The Maid of Munster.   1847: Jy 29;
     1851: Feb 12; 1852: Sept 25 (MH); 1857: Mar 2;
     1862: May 1, May 5; 1865: Jan 19; 1867: May 20.
     See also 392.
509. Persecuted Dutchman, The.   1864: Jy 4; 1867: Feb 22.
510. Personation.   1848: Apr 28, May 1; 1849: Oct 13.
511. Pet of the Petticoats.   1867: Mar 6, Apr 16.

512. Peter. 1849: Oct 31.
513. Peter Piper Pepper Podge. 1860: Jan 11, Jan 12;
     1863: Apr 2.
514. Pilgrim of Love. 1852: Oct 13 (MH); 1860: Mar 23.
515. Pirate Bride, The. 1857: Mar 16.
516. Pirate's Legacy, The 1867: Nov 9.
517. Pizarro. 1852: Nov 2; 1860: Dec 21; 1864: Nov 26;
     [...or The Death of Rollo]. 1832: May 17
     (Mansion House); 1847: Je 8; 1867: Mar 23;
     [...or The Spaniards in Peru]. 1847: Aug 5;
     1861: Nov 2.
518. Pleasant Neighbor, A or There's Nothing Like
     Leather. 1847: Je 26; 1852: Nov 24; 1853: Jy 30
     (MH); 1860: Jan 4; 1864: Sept 17; 1866: Nov 13.
519. Poacher's Doom, The. 1861: Dec 7; 1864: Sept 23.
     See also 734.
520. Po-ca-hon-tas. 1860: Oct 23, Oct 24, Oct 25; 1865:
     May 1, May 3; 1867: Apr 24.
521. Policy Ticket. 1861: Dec 2.
522. Poor Gentleman. 1851: Feb 27.
523. Poor of New York, The. 1861: Nov 25, Nov 26,
     Nov 28, Nov 29.
524. Poor Pillicody. 1851: Jan 23, Jan 28; 1853: Oct 28;
     1856: Je 30.
525. Popping The Question. 1863: Feb 28 (LH).
526. Post Boy, The. 1860: Aug 24, Aug 25 (LH).
527. Presumptive Evidence or Murder Will Out. 1847:
     Je 23.
528. Pretty House Breaker. 1867: Mar 25.
529. Pretty Milliners, The. 1865: Apr 4.
530. Putnam, The Iron Son of '76. 1847: Jy 5; 1851:
     Feb 6, Feb 7, Feb 8, Feb 24, Feb 25; 1862:
     Apr 21; 1865: Jan 11, Feb 11, Feb 22.
531. Pyramids, The. 1865: Apr 3.

532. Queen's Own or The Eccentric Lover. 1848: May 15;
     1849: Dec 25*; 1852: Oct 6 (MH). See also 152.
533. Quiet Family, The. 1866: Dec 14, Dec 17, Dec 18.

534. Race for a Diver, A. 1847: Dec 28.
535. Raffaelle or The Reprobate of Paris. 1864: Nov 15,
     Nov 22.
536. Rag Picker of Paris, The. 1864: Nov 18.
537. Raising the Wind. 1847: Je 7; 1854: Feb 1 (WH).

538. Rake's Progress. 1851: Feb 22; 1856: Jy 5.
539. Raoul or The Magic Star. 1863: May 1, May 2.
540. Rath Road or The Biters Bit. 1847: Aug 5.
541. Rebel or The Death Fetch of the Doomed. 1851: Feb 28. See also 542.
542. Rebel Chief or The Death Fetch. 1867: May 17, May 18. See also 541.
543. Rebel's Aricle. 1861: Dec 13, Dec 14.
544. Red Cow, The. 1866: May 18.
545. Regular Fix. 1865: Mar 23.
546. Rendezvous, The. 1865: Apr 5; [...or All in the Dark]. 1847: Jy 28; 1848: May 10; [... or Hide and Seek]. 1832: May 12 (Mansion House).
547. Rent Day. 1851: Jan 31; 1852: Oct 11 (MH).
548. Retired Chemist, The. 1856: Jan 14, Jan 15.
549. Returned Volunteer. 1864: Sept 3, Sept 15.
550. Review or The Humors of Irish Haymakers. 1849: Dec 19.
551. Review or The Wags of Windsor. 1847: Jy 9. See also 695.
552. Revolutionists and Royalists. 1866: Jy 4**.
553. Revolving Barrel, The. 1863: Apr 22.
554. Richard the III. 1832: May 16 (Mansion House); 1847: Jy 6 (Act 5), Jy 8 (Act 5), Aug 14, Dec 23 (Act 5), Dec 25 (Act 5); 1849: Oct 13; 1851: Feb 3 Oct 2; 1852: Aug 13 (Act 5), Oct 25 (MH), Nov 4; 1853: Aug 2 (MH); 1854: Jan 17; 1861: Sept 12; 1864: Dec 21, Dec 31 (Act 5, On horseback); 1865: Feb 18, Mar 22; 1866: Dec 29; 1867: Mar 8, Mar 23 (Act 5), Nov 16.
555. Richelieu or The Conspiracy. 1848: May 3; 1852: Sept 23 (MH); 1857: Nov 23; 1867: Oct 4.
556. Richelieu at 16. 1867: May 10.
557. Rip Van Winkle. 1865: Jan 6.
558. Rival Lovers. 1864: Nov 16.
559. Rivals, The. 1857: Aug 3, Aug 4, Aug 5; 1863: Feb 6 (LH).
560. Road into Pennsylvania, The. 1863: Nov 16, Nov 17, Nov 18.
561. Rob Roy or Auld Lang Syne. 1848: May 24; 1849: Dec 20, Dec 21; 1860: Dec 24; 1861: Nov 23; 1862: Mar 21, Mar 31; 1864: Dec 17; 1865: Apr 1; 1866: Dec 15.
562. Robber of the Rhine, The. 1863: Nov 2.
563. Robbers, The or The Forests of Bohemia. 1864: Dec 23; 1867: Feb 2, Oct 5.

564. Robber's Wife. 1832: May 19 (Mansion House); 1849: Dec 21; 1852: Aug 9 (MH); 1865: Jan 28; 1867: May 3.
565. Robert Emmet. 1860: Mar 17; 1862: Mar 18, Apr 1.
566. Robert Le Diable, Opera of. 1864: Sept 24 (Academy of Music).
567. Robert Macaire or The Two Murders. 1847: Jy 10; 1851: Feb 18; 1853: Jy 28 (MH); 1861: Dec 19; 1863: Apr 6 (Pantomime); 1864: Sept 23, Sept 28; 1865: Je 10; 1867: Oct 5, Nov 28.
568. Rockwood or Dick Turpin, the Highwayman. 1851: Feb 14, Feb 15. See also 132.
569. Roland for an Oliver, A. 1847: Mar 17; 1860: May 23.
570. Roll of the Drum. 1862: Mar 10, Mar 11.
571. Romance of a Poor Young Man. 1863: Apr 10.
572. Romantic Widow. 1851: Feb 17.
573. Romeo and Juliet. 1847: Jy 27; 1849: Nov 5 (LH) (Love Scene); 1852: Nov 1; 1865: Dec 11.
574. Rory O'More. 1861: Nov 2; 1865: Apr 21; 1867: Apr 8, Apr 9.
575. Rosina Meadows or Temptation Unveiled. 1852: Dec 23, Dec 24; 1858: Jy 17; 1861: Dec 25; 1865: Mar 13.
576. Rot or Cricket on the Hearth. 1864: Dec 25.
577. Rough Diamond. 1852: Oct 9 (MH); 1854: Jan 27 (WH); 1856: Jy 7; 1857: Mar 9; 1862: Mar 21; 1864: Dec 16, Dec 17; 1865: Jan 11, Jan 12, Feb 10; 1866: May 18, Nov 14; 1867: Apr 5, Apr 6.
578. Ruffian Boy. 1852: Nov 19.
579. Rush-In Bell. 1863: Nov 10, Nov 11.
580. Ruy Blas or The Lackey. 1865: Feb 17.

581. Sailor Boy's Dream. 1832: May 17 (Mansion House) (Recitation).
582. Sailor of France, The. 1857: Mar 6.
583. St. Mark, The Soldier of Fortune. 1867: Jan 23, Jan 25.
584. Sam Slick, The Clockmaker. 1847: Je 7.
585. Sandy and Jenny. 1863: Nov 12, Nov 13, Nov 14, Nov 26.
586. Sarah's Young Man. 1865: May 27, May 30.
587. Satan in Paris or The Mysterious Stranger. 1864: Sept 14; 1865: Feb 20. See also 447.

588. School for Scandal. 1853: Oct 31 (Readings from), Nov 2 (Scenes from); 1866: Nov 16.
589. School Master, The. 1863: Mar 4, Mar 5, Mar 6.
590. Sea of Ice or A Thirst for Gold. 1865: Mar 16, Mar 17.
591. Sea Side Story, A or Circumstantial Evidence. 1851: Feb 22.
592. Second Love. 1857: Feb 6.
593. Secret. 1854: Jan 26; 1856: Jy 11; 1860: Jan 7.
594. Secret, The [...or A Hole in the Wall]. 1847: Je 18, Je 29; [...or Mischievous Thomas]. 1864: Nov 5. See also 243 and 646.
595. Secret, The or Jealous Wife. 1848: May 13. See also 292.
596. Secret Marriage, The. 1865: Apr 3.
597. Secret Service of the United States. 1864: Dec 9.
598. Sent to the Tower. 1860: Jan 6, Jan 7.
599. Serious Family. 1852: Aug 3, Aug 4, Aug 7, Aug 11, Aug 21, Sept 30 (MH); 1853: Jy 6, Jy 7, Jy 8 (MH); 1856: Je 25; 1865: Mar 1; 1867: Apr 15.
600. Shakespeare Miscellany. 1850: Jan 24 (LH).
601. She Hunter of the Alps. 1853: Jy 28 (MH).
602. Shipwrecked Sailor, The. 1863; Mar 18, Mar 21.
603. Show Your Colors or Stars and Stripes. 1861: Dec 23.
604. Shundy McGuire. 1865: Mar 9.
605. Sicilian Pirate, The. 1866: Dec 15.
606. Singing and Dancing. 1855: Dec 14.
607. Six Degrees of Crime, The. 1862: Mar 15, Mar 19; 1864: Oct 1.
608. Sketches in India. 1851: Jan 30, Jan 31; 1857: Jan 22; 1865: Feb 28; 1866: Nov 30; 1867: Apr 15, Apr 24, Nov 18, Nov 19, Nov 28*.
609. Slasher and Crasher. 1852: Dec 2, Dec 4; 1854: Jan 11, Jan 14; 1860: Dec 21; 1864: Nov 14; 1865: Jan 14, Mar 11, May 1; 1867: Jan 12.
610. Smile. 1865: May 5.
611. Smoke Behind the Clouds. 1862: Jan 13.
612. Soldier's Daughter, The. 1847: May 15; 1865: May 30.
613. Soldier's Return from the War, The. 1856: Jy 1; 1857: Nov 26*.
614. Solon Shingle. 1864: Nov 21; 1867: Jan 14, Jan 15, Jan 17, Jan 18, Jan 19.
615. Somnambula, La, Opera of. 1855: Apr 27; 1860: Aug 20; 1864: Apr 25, Apr 26, Apr 27, Apr 28 (LH).

616. Somnambulist. 1856: Jy 7.
617. Son of the Wood, The or Robber's Life and Robber's
    Love. 1851: May 17.
618. Sons of Freedom and Daughters of Liberty, The. 1861:
    Oct 7, Oct 8.
619. Sorcerers. 1865: Apr 28 (LH).
620. Southern Smash-Up, The. 1863: Nov 21, Nov 23.
621. Spectre Bridegroom, The or A Ghost in Spite of
    Himself. 1832: May 11 (Mansion House); 1848:
    May 6, May 16, May 26; 1851; Feb 6, Feb 7,
    Mar 1; 1852: Aug 3, Aug 6 (MH); 1853: Jy 6,
    Jy 7 (MH), Nov 3; 1865: Jan 18, Jan 19, Jan 30;
    1867: Feb 9, Feb 11, Feb 12, Apr 25, Apr 27,
    Oct 1.
622. Spitfire, The. 1847: Je 22, Jy 8.
623. Spoil'd Child. 1832: May 8 (Mansion House).
624. Sprigs of Ireland. 1847: Je 29; 1849: Oct 8, Oct 19;
    1852: Oct 13 (MH).
625. Sprigs of Laurel or The Rival Soldiers. 1832: May 16
    (Mansion House).
626. Stage Struck Heroes, The. 1863: Apr 10.
627. Stage Struck Lawyer. 1856: Jan 16, Jan 17.
628. Star. 1865: Apr 4.
629. State Secrets. 1851: Jan 22.
630. Still Waters Run Deep. 1855: Nov 19, Nov 20;
    1864: Nov 4; 1865: May 27.
631. Stolen Sisters or A Tale of the Mohawk. 1857:
    Mar 16, Mar 19.
632. Stranger, The. 1847: Apr 10, Apr 14, May 10,
    May 29; 1849: Oct 10, Oct 31; 1851: Jan 30;
    1852: Nov 18, Nov 19; 1854: Jan 10, Jan 20;
    1861: Dec 6; 1862: Mar 14; 1865: Jan 25, Nov 15;
    1866: Dec 14; [...or Misanthropy and Repentance].
    1832: May 9 (Mansion House); 1866: Nov 12.
633. Streets of New York, The. 1865: Jan 9, Jan 10, Feb
    9; 1866: Dec 28.
634. Surprise Party, The. 1863: Apr 6.
635. Sweethearts and Wives. 1850: Aug 17; 1854: Jan 12,
    Jan 20.
636. Swiss Cottage, The. 1847: Je 11; 1849: Dec 7;
    1853: Jy 29 (MH); 1854: Feb 1 (WH); 1860: Dec 22;
    1864: Sept 6; 1867: Apr 13, Apr 17.
637. Swiss Swains, The. 1856: Jy 17; 1864: Sept 14.
638. Sylphide or The Dew Drop. 1847: Aug 16, Aug 18,
    Aug 21.

639. Tailor of Tamworth. 1866: May 24, May 29.
640. Tale of Blood. 1862: Apr 2.
641. Teddy the Tiller. 1849: Oct 20, Oct 23, Dec 18.
642. Temptation or The Irish Emigrant. 1867: Apr 29,
     Apr 30. See also 272.
643. Temptations. 1865: Apr 22.
644. Ten Nights in a Bar Room. 1860: Dec 1; 1865:
     Mar 18; 1866: Mar 24.
645. That Blessed Baby. 1856: Je 23.
646. That Rascal Tom or A Hole in the Wall. 1857: Nov
     28. See also 243 and 594.
647. Theresa's Vow. 1857: Nov 24.
648. Therese or Orphan of Genoa. 1847: Je 26; 1848:
     May 13; 1849: Oct 24, Nov 1; 1866: Dec 1. See
     also 484.
649. Third Night of the Marble Heart or The Sculpture's
     Dream. 1857: Jan 22.
650. Three Brothers, The. 1852: Nov 23.
651. Three Fast Girls. 1861: Nov 30.
652. Three Fast Men. 1865: Apr 1, Apr 8; [...or Female
     Minstrels]. 1865: Mar 4, Mar 31; [...or Life in
     New York]. 1864: Aug 29, Aug 30; 1865: Feb 8,
     Feb 11, Feb 22.
653. Three Guardsmen or The Queen, The Cardinal, and
     The Adventure. 1865: Mar 30.
654. Three Years after the Mysteries. 1849: Oct 25.
655. Ticket-of-Leave Man, The. 1864: Sept 8, Sept 9,
     Sept 10, Sept 12, Sept 17, Sept 28; 1865: Mar 8;
     1866: Apr 26 (Green Street Hall); 1867: Jan 8,
     Jan 11, Jan 21, Nov 26, Nov 27, Nov 28**.
656. Ticket-of-Leave Woman, The. 1864: Dec 9, Dec 16.
657. Times in Old Virginia or Yankee Pedaler. 1852:
     Dec 21.
658. Tom and Jerry or Life in London. 1832: May 19
     (Mansion House).
659. Tom Cringle. 1851: Jan 24, Jan 25; 1865: Jan 7,
     Jan 20.
660. Tom Moody's Secret. 1851: Feb 18.
661. Toodles, The. 1851: May 31, Je 2; 1852: Nov 8,
     Nov 15; 1856: Je 23, Jy 2; 1857: Mar 10; 1860:
     Nov 29; 1864: Sept 23; 1865: Mar 18 (LH)
     (Tipsey Scene); 1867: Jan 17, Jan 19.
662. Treble Artere. 1865: Apr 4.
663. Trip to California, A. 1852: Dec 17.
664. Trip to Richmond. 1864: Dec 30; 1865: Jy 8.

665. Turn Out or The Enraged Politician. 1832: Mar 17
    (Mansion House); 1851: Jan 22.
666. Turning of the Tables or The Knowing One Outwitted.
    1845: Jan 23 (Show Boat); 1851: Jan 29, Feb 3.
667. Turnpike Gate. 1832: May 12 (Mansion House);
    1851: Jan 20.
668. Two Bonnycastles. 1852: Oct 11 (MH); 1857: Feb 21,
    Mar 3, Mar 4.
669. Two Buzzards, The. 1861: Dec 9, Dec 10, Dec 19,
    Dec 25*; 1862: Mar 18; 1865: Je 8; 1867: Jan 9.
670. Two- Four- Five- Zero. 1851: Feb 8; 1861: Dec 4.
671. Two Friends, The. 1847: Je 11.
672. Two Gregories, The. 1845: Je 25 (Show Boat);
    1847: May 19, May 22, May 31; 1848: May 11.
673. Two-One- Five- Zero. 1861: Dec 4.
674. Two Pompeys, The. 1855: Apr 28.
675. Two Queens. 1858: Apr 1.
676. Two Wrestlers, The. 1865: Apr 11.

677. Uncle Sam. 1847: Jy 5. See also 448.
678. Uncle Tom's Cabin. 1853: Aug 15, Aug 16, Aug 17,
    Aug 18, Aug 19, Aug 20, Aug 22, Aug 23, Aug 24,
    Aug 25, Aug 26, Aug 27, Aug 30, Aug 31, Sept
    1 (MH); 1854: Jan 2*, Jan 3*, Jan 4, Jan 5, Jan 6, Jan 7,
    Jan 9; 1855: Je 4, Je 5, Je 6, Je 7 (WH), Nov 5,
    Nov 8; 1859: Oct 14, Oct 15, Oct 16, Oct 17, Oct
    18, Oct 19, Oct 21, Oct 22, Oct 23, Oct 24, Nov
    24**Nov 26**, Dec 12; 1860: Jan 2; 1861: Nov 18,
    Nov 19, Dec 25*; 1862: Mar 3, Mar 4, Mar 5 (?),
    Mar 6 (?), Mar 7, Mar 8**, Mar 10, Mar 13 (?),
    Mar 15, Mar 22, Mar 29; 1864: Sept 19, Sept 20,
    Sept 21; 1865: Jan 1, Feb 22, Mar 18, May 6*,
    Dec 23*; 1866: Nov 26, Nov 27, Nov 28, Nov 29**,
    Dec 8; 1867: Jan 7, Oct 14, Oct 15, Oct 16,
    Oct 17, Oct 18, Oct 19, Oct 21, Oct 22, Oct 23,
    Oct 24.
679. Union Bay and Pomp. 1865: Je (?).
680. Union Spy (or Scout), The or Pauline of the Cumber-
    land. 1865: Jy 1.
681. Unwelcome Visitor, The. 1863: Nov 16, Nov 17,
    Nov 18.
682. Upper Ten and Lower Million. 1862: Jan 18.

683. Vasco Peres. 1861: Dec 21, Dec 23.
684. Venice Preserved. 1847: May 27, Jy 28.
685. Vermont Wool Dealer. 1852: Aug 5, Aug 6 (MH).
686. Victims, The. 1867: Jan 18.
687. Victorine or "I'll Sleep On It". 1832: May 11, May 12
     (Mansion House); 1852: Dec 14, Dec 15.
688. Violet. 1865: Jan 27.
689. Virginia Cupids. 1847: Mar 4; 1849: Nov 3.
690. Virginia Mummy. 1847: Apr 14; 1849: Oct 26, Oct 30.
     1862: Mar 17.
691. Virginius or The Roman Father. 1847: Aug 9, Aug
     18; 1848: May 23; 1852: Oct 23 (MH); 1861: Oct 28.
692. Vision of Death. 1865: Apr 29.
693. Vision of the Dead. 1864: Sept 24.
694. Vol au Vent. 1863: Apr 13; 1865: Apr 4, Apr 7*.

695. Wags of Windsor. [1815: Dec 11; 1816: May 1]. See
     also 551.
696. Waiting for the Verdict. 1864: Dec 26; 1867: Feb 13,
     Feb 14.
697. Wallace, The Hero of Scotland. 1864: Dec 31.
698. Wandering Boys. 1847: Sept 3; 1851: Feb 20, Feb 28;
     1852: Oct 4, Oct 22 (MH); 1865: May 4.
699. Wandering Boys or The Castle or Olivil. 1832: May 8
     (Mansion House).
700. Wandering Boys of Switzerland. 1847: Jy 6, Jy 7.
701. Wandering Day or The Rose of Killarney. 1865:
     Mar 2.
702. Wandering Minstrel, The. 1856: Je 25; 1866: Dec 29;
     1867: Oct 2, Oct 3.
703. Warlock of the Glen or The Rightful Heir of Glen-
     cairn. 1848: May 8, May 22; 1849: Dec 7; 1852:
     Nov 29; 1865: Jan 21.
704. Warning and Ronslaus. 1852: Nov 30.
705. Waterman, The. 1847: Dec 23, Dec 25*.
706. Way to Get Married. [1813: Oct 5, Oct 6].
707. Weathercock, The or Lover's Metamorphosis. 1848:
     May 1, May 3.
708. Wept of the Wish-Ton-Wish, The. 1864: Sept 30;
     1867: Nov 21, Nov 23. See also 452.
709. Werner. 1857: Mar 14.
710. White Boys of Ireland or The Heroine of Galaway.
     1865: Jan 18.
711. Whites and Browns. 1852: Aug 20 (MH).
712. Who Do They Take Me For? 1848: May 8.

713. Who Speaks First! 1851: Dec 16.
714. Widow's Victim, The or The Stage Struck Barber.
    1847: Je 17, Je 21, Aug 12; 1849: Oct 22, Oct 23;
    1852: Sept 28, Oct 19 (MH), Nov 17; 1856: Jy 8,
    Jy 12; 1861: Dec 4; 1862: Mar 14; 1865: Mar 18
    (LH); 1867: Nov 8. See also 298.
715. Wife, The or A Tale of Mantua. 1847: Apr 12,
    May 20; 1848: May 9.
716. Wife A Day. 1852: Oct 23 (MH).
717. Wife For a Day. 1852: Nov 20; 1854: Jan 27 (WH).
718. Wife for Half an Hour, A. 1864: Nov 7, Nov 8,
    Nov 9.
719. Wife's First Lesson, A. 1847: Jy 27. See also
    123.
720. Wife's Revenge. 1851: Feb 24, Feb 25.
721. Wild Oats. 1867: Jan 25.
722. Willful Murder. 1861: Nov 1.
723. William Tell. 1859: Nov 10. See also 724 and 24.
724. William Tell or The Hero of Switzerland. 1847: Jy
    30, Aug 4; 1862: May 1; 1866: Dec 1. See also
    (?) 723 and 24.
725. Willow Corpse. 1864: Nov 5; 1865: Jan 14, Jan 18,
    Jan 30.
726. Winning a Husband. 1852: Nov 1, Nov 4.
727. Winter's Tale. 1857: Feb 19, Feb 20 (Statue Scene).
728. Wizard at the Moor. 1862: Mar 20.
729. Wizard of the Glen or Spirits of the Black Mantel.
    1849: Nov 29.
730. Wizard of the North. 1852: Oct 18 (MH).
731. Wizard Skiff. 1865: Feb 28; [The Fairy Skiff]. 1867:
    Nov 20.
732. Woman, Her Love, Her Fate, Her Trials. 1851:
    Feb 19, Feb 21.
733. Woman's Love. 1853: Aug 2 (MH).
734. Woman's Trials. 1862: Mar 22; [... or The Poacher's
    Doom]. 1865: Jan 21, Feb 23. See also 519.
735. Woman's Whims. 1865: May 5; 1867: Nov 16.
736. Wonder, The or Woman Keeps a Secret. 1847: May
    21, May 29.
737. Wool Pedlar. 1847: Je 5.
738. Wreckers, The. 1857: Feb 18.

739. Yankee Cheese or Love and Buttermilk. 1857:
    Mar 21.
740. Yankee Duelist. 1854: Jan 26, Jan 31 (WH); 1861:
    Dec 3; 1862: Mar 20.

741. Yankee Farmer. 1852: Dec 1.
742. Yankee Land or The Founding of the Apple Orchard.
     1847: Je 3.
743. Yankee Outwilled. 1861: Dec 13.
744. Yankee Outwitted in Newark, The. 1857: Mar 16,
     Mar 17.
745. Yankee Peculiarities. 1846: Feb 27, Feb 28
     (Franklin Hall).
746. Young Actress, The. 1864: Sept 2, Sept 17, Dec 31.
747. Young America. 1845: Je 25 (Show Boat).
748. Young Scamp or My Grandfather's Pet. 1847: Jy 7,
     Jy 10; 1852: Aug 5, Aug 11, Oct 8, Oct 9 (MH).
749. Young Widow, The or A Lesson for Lovers . . .
     1832: May 8 (Mansion House); 1847: Aug 6;
     1849: Oct 6, Oct 26.
750. Youth Who Never Saw a Woman, The. 1852: Nov 23;
     1864: Sept 17, Nov 22; 1867: Jan 30.
751. Youthful Queen, The or Christina of Sweden. 1847:
     May 3; 1848: Apr 27.
752. Your Life's in Danger. 1857: Feb 17; 1867: Feb 15,
     Feb 16.

753. Zarah or The Gypsey Queen. 1857: Mar 18.
754. Zoe, The Octoroon or Life in Louisiana. 1864: Nov 10,
     Nov 11, Nov 16. See also 475.

Appendix B

List of Players

1. Adams, Mrs. 1856: Mar 24 #.

2. Addams, A. A. 1832: May 14 (120), 15 (280), 16
   (552), 17 (517), 19 (486, 658, 554); 1847: Aug 6
   (281), 10 (46), 14 (555), 18 (691), 20 (325), 21
   (120), 23 # (385), 25 (385), Sept 6 (385); 1848:
   May 11 (486), 15, 16 (70), 18 #, 25 (120).

3. Addison, Miss Laura 1851: Dec 15 (408), 16 (339).

4. Albaugh, J. W. 1865: Dec 11 (573); 1867: Jan 28- 29
   (492), 30 (159), 31 (447), Feb 1 (150), 2 # (563,
   321).

5. Albertine, Miss 1851: May 31; 1856: Jy 8, 9 (288,
   456), 10 (204, 507).

6. Alexander 1862: Mar 3 (678)+.

7. Allen 1861: Dec 24 (120), 26 (120).

8. Allen, J. H. 1853: Jy 25, Aug 2 #.

9. Anderson 1851: Feb 12, 14 (440), 18 (660), 19 (455),
   21 (456).

10. Averill, Mrs. 1850: Aug 17.

11. Baldwin 1853: Jy 2+.

12. Bannister, Mrs. 1851: Feb 19 (455), 21 (455), 24- 25
    (530).

13. Barnes, Miss Charlotte (see also Conner, Mrs. E. S.)
    1847: May 3 (751), 6, 7 (339), 8 (253), 10 # (44,
    632, 11 (177), 12 (253), 13 (339, 245), 14 # (177),
    18 (413), 19 (486), 20 (715), 22 (245, 82), 25 (156),
    26 (82, 339), 27 # (684, 19), 28 (56, 321), 29 (632,
    736), Je 1 (229), 9 (339), Jy 27 (573), 28 (684), 31
    (138, 165), Aug 2 (368, 19), 4 (120), 5 (517), 7
    (245, 81), 9 (691, 283), 12 # (229), 25 (385, 283).

14. Barrett, George 1847: Je 11 (671, 241).

15. Barrett, Joseph 1866: Nov 1+; 1867: Feb 25- 28, Mar 1- 2 (42).

16. Barrett, Mrs. Viola 1866: Nov 8- 10 (364), Dec 13 (486); 1867: Feb 4- 8 (475), 25- 28, Mar 1- 2 (42), Apr 15 # (599, 608), 24 (520, 608).

17. Battershall 1851: Feb 26 (502); 1854: Jan 14- 16 (262).

18. Beam, Miss Fannie 1861: Nov 18- 19 (678).

Belcour, Mrs. See Thorne and Mestayer

19. Bellamy, Mrs. 1857: Feb 17 (229).

20. Bland, Humphrey 1864: Dec 12- 14 (43).

21. Bleeker 1847: Je 16 (80, 231).

22. Blue. Miss Ginge 1849: Oct 12 #, 26+, 30 (690).

23. Boon Children 1853: Nov 2 (165, 325, 146, 588, 290).

24. Boon, Miss Lora Gordon 1853: Nov 3 (229).

25. Boulet, M. and Mmd. 1847: Jy 2 (137, 182), 5 (182).

26. Bowers, Mrs. D. P. 1867: Mar 11- 12 (338), 13 (262, 473), 14 (473, 150), 15 # (338, 296), 16 (346, 45).

27. Bradshaw 1853: Aug 22- 27 (678).

28. Brandon, J. M. 1847: Apr 9+; 1848: May 24 #.

28A. Brennan, T. 1859: Oct 14- 19 (678), 21- 24 (678).

29. Brown, S. 1853: Oct 25 (253), 27 (339), Nov 3 (335).

30. Browne 1850: Je 22 (141, 198).

31. Browne, S. E. 1854: Jan 2- 7 (679), 9 (679), 10 (371, 632), 11 (380), 12 (291, 635), 13 (380, 406), 14- 16 (262), 17 # (553), 27 (557, 717, 279).

32. Bryant, Dan 1867: Apr 29- 30 (642, 231), May 1 (59, 432), 2 (276, 432, 158), 3 # (241, 158, 564), 4 (241, 121, 415).

33. Buchanan 1858: Jy 31 (486); 1859: Mar 14 (204); 1864: Dec 19 (385), 20 (229), 21 (555), 22 (486), 23 (563).

34. Buchanan, Virginia 1864: Dec 19 (385), 20 (229), 21 (554), 22 (486).

34A. Buckbee, E. 1859: Feb 16 (139).

35. Burgess 1853: Mar 21 (385); 1854: Jan 11 (380), 12 (291), 13 (380), 14-16 (262), 17 (554), 20 (632), 21 (348).

36. Burke, William 1854: Jan 10 (371, 632), 12 (635), 14-16 (262), 20 (622, 635), 21 (348); 1857: Jan 22 (649), Feb 5 (262); 1860: Mar 17 (565), Nov 29 (140, 661), Dec 19, 21 (610), 22 (636).

37. Burke, Mrs. William 1860: Jan 4-5 (111), 6 (286), 7 (467), Mar 17 (565).

38. Burke, W. E. 1857: Jan 22 (608).

39. Burton, W. E. 1856: Je 23 (661, 645), 24, 25 (599, 702), 28, 30 (524, 287), Jy 2 (661, 54), 4, 5 (538).

40. Butler, Bob (1863: Mar 4-6 (589), 21 (602), May 1 #

41. Byrne 1847: Oct 7 (376).

42. Cantor 1861: Nov 7-9 (475).

43. Carman 1853: Jy 25.

44. Carman, Laura 1853: Jy 25, 28 #.

45. Carmen, Louise 1867: Feb 25-28 (42), Mar 1-2 (41).

46. Carpenter, Miss 1847: Jy 28 (546), 30 (120), Aug 23 (385), 25 (385), Sept 6 (385).

47. Carroll, Mrs. 1848: Jan 27-28 (104).

48. Carter 1861: Nov 11-14 (240).

49. Cartlitch, J. G. 1852: Dec 16 #.

50. Chanfrau, F. S. 1847: Je 16 (80), 17 (714), 25 #, Jy 8 (410) 12 #, Aug 12 (229, 298); 1848: May 26 (214, 621, 367, 123); 1849: Oct 22 (714, 433), 23 (125, 641, 714, 433), 24 (214, 648), 25 # (49, 426, 654, 424); 1850: Je 19-22, Oct 5 (137, 90), 7 (339, 426); 1851: May 31 (433); 1852: Nov 8, 15 (661), 16 (137), 17; 1856: Jy 8 (714), 9 (288, 456), 10 (204, 507), 12.

51. Chapman, C. 1853: Oct 25 (253, 461), 27 (339).

52. Chapman, Miss 1853: Oct 25 (461).

53. Chapman, Miss Caroline 1850: Jy 15 (378, 165),
    Aug 17.

54. Chapman, F. M. 1864: Oct 3 (146).

55. Chapman, George 1849: Oct 5 (125), 8 (133), 23
    (714), 24 (133), 31 (512), Dec 7 (636); 1850: Jy 15 #,
    Nov 2 (84).

56. Chapman, Mrs. George 1849: Oct 12 #, Dec 7 (410,
    636), 8 #, 23 (2); 1850: Je 22 (141, 198), Jy 10
    (80), 15 #.

57. Chapman, Miss Mary 1849: Oct 8 (624), 13; 1850:
    Jy 10 (138).

58. Chapman, W. B. 1850: Aug 17.

59. Charles 1865: Apr 21 (574).

60. Charles, G. C. 1860: Mar 22 (269, 278), 23 (514),
    24 (269, 399), [26 # ?].

61. Charles, H. A. 1851: Oct 1 (395, 241), 2 (554).

62. Chesborough 1852: Dec 17 #.

    Chipp. See Thorne and Mestayer

63. Ciucre, Miles. 1856: Jy 14 (292).

64. Clark 1865: Mar 21 (385).

65. Clark, Conrad 1857: Feb 5 (262).

66. Clark, N. B. 1850: Oct 26 (140), Nov 2 (84); 1851:
    Jan 20 (55), 23 (55), 24 (55, 659), 25 (183, 659),
    29 (486), 31 (547), Feb 3 (554), 4 (229), 5 (339),
    6-8 (530), 10-11 (414), 22 (538), 24-25 (530), 26 #
    (84, 502).

67. Clark, W. C. 1861: Nov 11-14 (240), Dec 2 (160), 3
    (93), 4 (137), 5 (339), 6 (632, 93), 7 (484, 392,
    519).

68. Clarke 1861: Nov 11 (239), 13 (240).

69. Clarke, C. W. 1864: Nov 2 (160), 3 (160, 114),
    4 (630), 5 (725), 7-9 (718), 10-11 (754), 12 (137),
    14 (609), 15 # (536, 140), 16 (754), 17 (111), 19
    (384), 21 (115), 22 (535), 25 (137), 26 (517), Dec
    19 (385); 1865: Jan 19 (160), 20 # (658, 354, 243),
    21 (354, 703, 164, 734).

70. Clarke, H. G.   1864: Dec 15 (412), 17 # (561), 31 (697); 1865: Jan 13 (339, 392), 14 (725, 471, 607), 18 (725), 30 (725, 621), Feb 13 (385), 14 (286), Apr 12 # (488).

71. Clarke, J. W.   1847: Je 23 (527).

72. Cline, Herr   1849: Nov 1 # (83).

72A. Cline, T. S.   1859: Feb 16 (139).

73. Cole, Miss Alice   1866: Nov 1+.

74. Cole, Miss Kate   1866: Nov 1+.

75. Conner   1847: Aug 23 (385), 25 (385), Sept 6 (385).

76. Conner, E. S.   1848: Apr 27 (339), 28 (376), 29, May 1 # (193), 2, 3, (555); 1849: Oct 10 (632), 11 (245, 2), 12 (253), 13 (554, 510), 15 # (474, 335); 1850: Jan 24.

77. Conner, Mrs. E. S.   (See also Barnes, Charlotte) 1848: Apr 27 (339), 28 (376), 29, May 1 # (193), 2, 3 (555), 4 (435); 1849: Oct 10 (632), 11 (245, 2), 12 (253), 13 (554, 510), 15 # (474, 335); 1850: Jan 24.

78. Conover   1847: Je 24 (148), Aug 12 (229).

79. Cooper   1847: Jy 29 (120), Aug 12 (229), 23 (385), 25 (385), Sept 6 (385).

80. Copland   1849: Oct 6 (749).

81. Cowell, Joe   1851: Jan 20 (55, 667), 22 (55), 23 (55, 524), 24 (55, 659), 25 (184, 659), 28 (524), 29 (666), 30 (632, 608), Feb 3 (666), 4 # (229), 5 (169), 6-8 (530), 10-11 (412, 54), 14 # (569, 441), 27 (522, 442).

82. Corrie, Millie   1859: Mar 14 (204), Ap 1 (140).

83. Crawford, Miss   1847: Aug 12 (229), 14 (146), 16 (178), 23 (385), Sept 3 (376, 698), 6 (385).

84. Cruise, Anna   1847: May 17 (569).

84A. Cunningham, H.   1859: Feb 16 (139).

85. Cushman, Miss Maj. Pauline   1864: Nov 28 (505, 351), Dec 5-7 (107), 8 (396), 9 # (597, 656), 1865: Mar 6-7 (505), 8 (656), 9 (47), 10 # (107), 11 (107), Jy 1 (680), 6 (185), Dec 25 (575); 1866: May 17 (105, 366), 23 (427, 72).

86. Daly, Julia 1859: Mar 5 (491).

87. D'Artist 1847: Jy 29 (508).

88. D'Auberval, Madame Mina 1865: Mar 21 (345, 331), 25 (95, 350);

89. Davenport, A. H. 1852: Sept 23 (555); 1853: Jy 2+; 1860: May 23 (201, 569), 26.

90. Davenport, E. L. 1861: Dec 24 (120), 26 (120); 1867: Jan 22 (229), 23 (583), 24 (171, 49), 25 # (583, 721), 26 (120, 49).

91. Davenport, H. 1865: Mar 18.

92. Davidge, William Jr. 1864: Nov 3 (160, 114); 1865: Mar 18 (714).

93. DeLorine, Miss 1847: May 17.

94. De Mall, Frank 1865: Mar 18.

95. Denin, Miss Kate (see also Ryan, Kate Denin) 1847: Je 19 (216), Jy 6 (700, 554), 7 (700), 8 (555); 1865: Jan 16-17 (150).

96. Denin, Susan 1847: Jy 6 (700, 554), 7 (748, 700), 8 (409, 554), 9 (51).

97. Denis 1852: Sept 23 (555).

98. Denvil, Miss (1860: Dec 19 (120), 21 (517), 22 (380).

99. Derr, W. R. 1851: Feb 6-8 (530), 10-11 (412), 12 # (418), 14 (568), 24-25 (530).

100. Derr, William 1862: Apr 21.

101. Diamond 1854: Feb 1 #.

102. Dickinson, G. K. 1857: Jan 22 (649), Feb 17 (229), 18 (738), 19 (74, 727), 20 (74, 727), 21 (210), Mar 16+#.

103. Dillon, Charles 1867: Jan 5.

103A. Doit 1859: Feb 16 (139), Mar 14 (204) (124).

104. Don, Lady 1867: Mar 25 (96, 528), 26 (506, 323), 27 (68, 323), 28 (468, 323), 29 # (137, 9), 30 (96, 9).

105. Donaldson 1853: Oct 25 (253), 27 (339), 28 (208).

106. Donnelly, T. L. 1866: Dec 17-18 (98, 449), 19 (226, 114), 20, 21 #, 22.

107. Donovan, Paddy 1864: Dec 3 (497).

108. Drew, Frank 1865: Jan 3-4 (1, 75, 231), 5 (272, 432), 6 (411, 559), 7 (432, 411).

109. Drew, Master F. 1847: Je 16 (232).

109A. Drew, I. N. 1859: Oct 14-19 (678), 21-24 (678).

110. Drew, J. N. 1866: Nov 1+.

111. Drum, George 1856: Mar 24 (140), 26 # (140).

112. Ducy - Barre 1856: Jy 14 (292).

113. Duff 1867: Oct 25-26 (480).

113A. Duff, James 1859: Oct 14-19 (678), 21-24 (678).

114. Durnat 1853: Jy 2+.

115. Dyott, Mrs. 1851: Feb 3 (554), 4 (229), 5 (339), 27 (522).

116. Eddy, Ed 1851: Jan 27, 28 (335), 29 (486), 30 (632), 31 (547), Feb 3 (554), 4 # (229, 276); 1861: Oct 28 (691, 28), 30 (286), 31 (335), Nov 1 # (341, 241), 2 (517, 574).

117. Evans 1852: Aug 16 (288).

118. Everdale, Miss 1853: Oct 21 (339), 29 (276).

119. Everett 1853: Jy 2+.

120. Eytinge, Miss Rose 1867: Feb 18-21 (226), 22 # (237), 23 (237).

121. Faye, Mons. 1865: Mar 25 (96, 350).

122. Ferris 1860: Dec 19 (120).

123. Fisher, Miss Kate 1864: Aug 24-26 (412), 29-30 (652), Sept 2 # (132, 746, 412), 3 (350), 8-10 (655), 12 (655), 14, 17, 26-28, 29 (204), 30, Oct 3 # (409, 106), Nov 7-9 (170), 10-11 (754), 16 (754), 19 (287), 22 (165), 24 (412, 132), 25 (204), 26 (412), Dec 15 412), 16 (656, 576), 24 (204), 31 (746, 555); 1865: Jan 1 (224), 9 (633, 132), 10 (635, 204), 11 (530, 577), 12 # (577, 268, 454), Feb 8 (652, 454), 9 (633, 449), 10 # (132, 577, 65), 11 (652, 530, 288), 22 (678, 530, 652), Mar 4 (652, 132), 11 (475), 13

(575, 225), 16-17 (590), 18 (644, 678, 288), 27-28 (94), 29 (85, 169), 30 (132, 653), 31 # (652, 178), Apr 8 (652, 84).

124. Fleming, William M.   1852: Sept 23 (555), 24 (339), 25 (364), 27 # (451); 1857: Nov 23.

125. Florance   1852: Dec 18 (86).

126. Floyd   1853: Jy 2+.

127. Forrest, Miss Kate   1860: Nov 29 (140)**.

128. Foster, Chas.   1861: Nov 7-9 (475), 18-19 (678); 1862: May 1 (725), 2 (486), 3 (245), 5 (508, 120).

129. Foster, W. M.   1855: Je 18-20 (364).

130. Foster, Mrs. W. M.   1855: Je 18-20 (364).

131. France, Miss A.   1860: Jan 6 (286), 7 (137).

131A. France, R.   1859: Feb 16 (139).

131B. France, R. G.   1859: Feb 16 (139).

131C. France, Shirley   1859: Feb 16 (139), Mar 14 (204) (124).

132. Frary, Mrs.   1847: Apr 9+.

133. Fredericks, W. S.   1847: Apr 9 (245, 279), 10 (632), 12 (715), 13 (486), 14 (632), 15 (339), May 7 (339), 8 (253), 10 (44, 632), 12 (253), 13 # (339, 245), 18 (413), 20 (715), 25 (156), 26 (339), 27 (684), 28 (156), 29 (736), Je 1 (229), 11 (671, 241), Jy 27 (573), 28 (684), 30 (120), Aug 2 (368), 5 (517), 7 # (245), 9 (691), 12 (229), 14 (554), 16 (177), 18 (691), 20 (325), 25 (283); 1849: Oct 12 (253).

134. Frost, Miss A.   1861: Nov 20-23 (501), Dec 2 (160), 24 (120), 26 (120).

135. Frost, A. J.   1849: Nov 3 (340), 20 #, 29 (729), Dec 7 # (703, 410, 636).

136. Gapin   1866: Nov 8-10 (364), 12 (632).

137. Germon, Miss Delly   1860: Nov 29 (140)**.

138. Germon, Mrs. G. C.   1860: Nov 29 (140)**.

139. Glassford   1867: Oct 25-26 (480).

139A. Glassford, A. 1859: Oct 14- 19 (678), 21- 24 (678).

139B. Glassford, Mrs. Jessie 1859: Oct 14- 19 (678), 21- 24 (678).

140. Glatigny, Mons. 1865: Mar 25 (95, 304, 350).

141. Glenn 1853: Jy 2+.

142. Gomersol 1864: Dec 26 (696, 52)+.

143. Gomersol, Mrs. 1864: Dec 26 (696, 52)+, 30 (96).

144. Goorlay 1850: Jy 10 (138).

145. Gossin, F. G. 1866: Nov 12 (632); 1867: Jan 8 (655), Feb 4- 8 (475)+, Mar 1 # (167), 2.

146. Gourlay 1851: May 31, Je 2.

147. Gratton, H. P. 1847: Apr 15 (339); 1848: May 9 (715), 11 (486), 15 (486).

148. Gratton, Mrs. H. 1852: Aug 20 (339).

148A. Grey, P. 1859: Mar 14 (204).

149. Griffith 1849: Oct 15 (475); 1850: Je 22 (198), Jy 10 (138, 80); 1852: Aug 20 (711), 21 #.

150. Griffiths, C. 1853: Jy 2+, 30 #.

151. Griffiths, Mrs. 1853: Jy 2+.

152. Grover, J. A. 1867: Feb 13, 14 (696).

153. Guion, H. D. 1865: Mar 18.

154. Hall, Harry 1857: Feb 5 (39), 17 (229), 18 (738), 19- 20 (371).

155. Hamilton 1867: Sept 28 (385), Oct 25- 26 (480), 30- 31 (365).

156. Hamilton 1850: Aug 17.

157. Hamilton, Mrs. 1850: Aug 17.

158. Hamilton, Mrs. Claudie 1867: Oct 28.

158A. Hamilton, T. 1859: Oct 14- 19 (678), 21- 24 (678).

158B. Hamilton, Mrs. T. 1859: Oct 14- 19 (678), 21- 24 (678).

159. Hann, T. 1852: Aug 20 (339).

160. Hardy, Mrs. 1867: Oct 25- 26 (480)+.

160A. Hardy, Miss Lizzie 1859: Oct 14- 19 (678), 21- 24 (678).

161. Harrison, Mrs. 1847: Apr 9+, May 17, Je 5 (49), 11 (671), 16 (80), Jy 1 (339), 28 (546), Aug 5 (517), 6 (281), 10 (46).

162. Harrison 1865: Apr 25- 26 (466).

163. Harrison, Mrs. 1865: Apr 25- 26 (466).

164. Harrison, Miss Alice A. 1865: Mar 18, 21 (385).

165. Harrison, G. W. 1866: Nov 8- 10 (364).

165A. Hart, B. 1859: Feb 16 (139), Mar 14 (204) (124).

166. Hauntonville, Mrs. 1849: Nov 29 # (735, 367).

167. Haviland, E. N. 1854: Jan 20 (632), 21 (301, 348); 1860: Mar 17 (565).

168. Hearne, J. A. 1867: Mar 8 (111, 554).

169. Henderson, Mrs. Ettie 1856: Jan 14- 17 (8), 22 (8), 24 (8).

170. Henderson, Wm. 1852: Sept 23 (554).

171. Hendricks, Miss Emma 1865: Mar 18.

172. Henricks, Miss 1865: Mar 18.

173. Herbert 1847: Apr 9+.

174. Herbert, Mrs. J. 1851: May 31, Je 2.

175. Herndon, T. J. 1864: Oct 3 (146).

176. Heron Family 1847: Dec 22 (478, 258, 279), 23, 24, 25, 28, 29.

177. Heron, Miss 1847: Dec 22 (478, 258, 279), 23, 24, 25 (332), 28, 29.

178. Heron, Miss F. 1847: Dec 22, 23, 24, 25 (333), 28, 29.

179. Heron, Matilda 1862: Apr 28 (74).

180. Herring, Miss Fannie 1865: Feb 20 (587, 360), 21 (384, 327), 23 (452, 734), 24 # (204, 297), 25 (204, 288, 269).

181. Hickey 1853: Nov 3 (621).

182. Hicks, George H. 1860: Nov 29 (140)**.

183. Higgins, W. G. 1865: Apr 25-26 (466), 29 (692, 467).

184. Higgins, W. S. 1864: Sept 19 (678), 20-21; 1866: Nov 8-10 (364).

185. Hill, Charles 1865: Je 9 (295, 242).

186. Hill, G. H. 1861: Dec 3 (740); 1862: Mar 17.

186A. Hilliard, C. 1859: Oct 14-19 (678), 21-24 (678).

187. Hitchcock, William 1863: May 13 (116, 58, 334).

188. Holmes 1853: Oct 25 (253, 460); 1860: Mar 17 (565).

189. Howard, Charles 1847: Je 3 (337), 4 (146), 5 (49), 7 (537), 11 (671, 636); 1850: Je 22 (141, 198), Jy 10 (138, 80), Aug 17; 1856: Je 24 (190, 296), 25, 28 (30), Jy 1 (44, 613), 4, 7 (616, 398, 577).

190. Howard, Mrs. Charles 1847: Je 3 (337), 4 (146), 7 (537), 11 (671, 636); 1850: Jy 10 (138); 1856: Je 24 (190, 296), 25, 29 (30), Jy 1 (44, 613), 5 (538), 7 # (616, 398, 577.

191. Howard, Miss Clara 1865: Mar 18.

192. Howard, G. C. 1855: Nov 5 (678), 8 (678), 9; 1859: Feb 16 (139), Nov 24 (678, 478)**, 26 (678, 478)**, Dec 12 (678); 1860: Jan 4-5 (111), 6 (286).

193. Howard, Little Cordelia 1855: Nov 5 (678), 8 (678), 9 #; 1859: Feb 16 (139), Nov 24 (678, 478)**, 26 (678, 478)**, Dec 12 (678); 1860: Jan 2 (678, 480).

194. Howard, Mrs. G. C. 1855: Nov 5 (678), 8 (678), 9; 1859: Feb 16 (139), Oct 14-18 # (678), 21-24 (678), Nov 24 (678, 478)**, 26 (678, 478)**, Dec 12 (678); 1860: Jan 2 (678, 480), 4-5 (111), 6 (286), 7 (137, 467); 1867: Oct 14-18 #-19* (678), 21-24 (678), 25 #-26 (480).

195. Hunt, H. B. 1847: May 4 (92), Je 11 (636), Aug 23 (385), 25 (385), Sept 6 (385); 1853: Nov 21 (238).

196. Hutchinson, R. B. 1852: Dec 24 #.

197. Hyde, Miss 1861: Nov 7-9 (475), 11-14 (240).

198. Irving, Henrietta 1865: May 29 (74).

199. Isaacs   1861: Nov 11-14 (240).

200. Jackson, A. W. Jr.   1847: Jy 1 (339).

201. Januaschek, Miss Fanny   1867: Dec 3 (409).

Janvia.   See Thorne and Mestayer.

202. Jeffers, W. W.   1865: Apr 12 (493).

203. Jefferson, Miss   1851: Jan 25 (659).

204. Jeffries   1861: Nov 11 (240), 13 (240).

205. Johnson   1852: Aug 16 (367).

206. Johnson, Miss   1853: Aug 22-27 (678).

207. Johnson, Miss Emma   1865: Jan 13 (339, 392), 14
     (725, 471, 609), 17 (471), 18 (725), 19 (160), 30
     (725, 621).

208. Johnston   1860: May 25 (111, 49), 26 #.

209. Johnston, R.   1857: Mar (173)+; 1858: Jy 31 (486).

210. Jones, R.   1851: May 31, Je 2.

211. Jones, Mrs. W. G.   1861: Oct 31 (335), Nov 1 (341).

212. Jordon, Mrs.   1864: Sept 22 (380).

213. Jordon, Mrs. H.   1865: Feb 13 (385), Jy 8 (49).

214. Jordan, H. C.   1855: Je 18-20 (384).

215. Jordon, Little Miss   1864: Sept 19 (678), 20-21.

216. Kames, G. S.   1864: Nov 7, 18 # (507, 536).

217. Kent, M. F.   1851: Feb 6-7 (530, 621), 8 (530).

218. Kerne, T. W.   1865: Jan 3-4 (1, 75, 231).

219. King, C. A.   1847: Apr 9+; 1851: Jan 20 (55), 23 (524),
     24 (55, 659), 25 (184, 659), 29 (486, 666), 31 (547),
     Feb 3 (554, 666), 4 (229), 5 (339), 10-11 (412),
     14 (440), 27 # (522).

219A. King, J. H.   1859: Mar 14 (204).

220. Kimberly, Miss   1861: Nov 4-6 (478), 7 (478, 240),
     8 # - 9 (478), 11-13 (288), 14 (288, 478), 15 # (229,
     446), 16 (210, 288).

221. Kneas   1851: May 31, Je 2.

222. Kunkel, Miss Addie   1865: Jan 23 (74), 24 (339), 25
     (632, 56), 26, 27 # (300, 688), 28 (300, 564), Feb
     1- 2 (94), 3 # (94), 4 (94)**, 6- 7 (94).

223. LaFond, Miss Florence   1864: Oct 3 (106).

224. La Forest, Mrs.   1847: Apr 9+, Aug 10 (46), Sept
     6 #.

225. Le Braun, Miss Virginia   1866: Nov 1+.

226. LeBrun Mrs. Eliza   1866: Nov 1+.

227. Le Roy, Miss Clara   1857: Mar 16+.

228. Lee, Miss   1861: Nov 16 (210).

229. Leffler, M.   1857: Mar 16+.

230. Lennox 1853: Aug 22- 27 (678).

     Lenox.   See Thorne and Mestayer.

231. Lester, Miss   1862: May 2 (486).

232. Lewis, Mrs. H.   1852: Nov 2 (517, 245), 3 (157, 49),
     4 (726, 554), 5 # (288, 204).

233. Linden, H.   1860: Jan 2 (480), 4 (518), 5, 6 (286,
     598), 7 (467, 598).

234. Lotta, Mlle.   1867: Apr 16 (511, 449), 17 (636, 169),
     18 (47, 78, 449), 19 # (179, 473), 22 (17, 220),
     23 (170).

235. Loveday   1862: Apr 28 (74), May 1 (508), 2 (486),
     3 (245), 5 (508), (120).

236. Lovell, H. V.   1851: Jan 18 (339), Feb 5 (339), 14
     (568), 15 (151), 17 (428, 572), 18 (567), 19 (732),
     21 (732), 22 (538, 591), 24- 25 (530), Mar 1 (23).

237. Lovell, Mrs. H. V.   1851: Jan 18 (339), 27, 28,
     (335), 29 (486), 30 (632, 608), 31 (547, 608),
     Feb 3 (554), 4 # (229, 276), 5 (339), 6- 8 (530),
     10- 11 (412, 54), 14 (568, 440), 15 (151), 17 (428,
     572), 18 (567, 660), 19 (455, 732), 20 (467, 698),
     21 (455, 722), 22 (538, 591), 24 # (530), 25 # (530),
     26 (84, 502), 28 (541, 698).

165

237A. McAuley, B.   1859: Feb 16 (139), Mar 14 (204).

238. McCollum, J. C.   1867: Mar 11-12 (338), 13 (262), 14 (150), 15 (338).

239. McDonald 1852: Aug 16 (413), Sept 23 (555), Nov 8 #.

240. McDonough 1847: Je 8 # (276).

241. McKean 1858: Jy 31 (486).

242. McMillin 1860: Dec 19, 21.

243. Macarthy, Mr. & Miss 1853: Jy 25.

244. MacGregor 1852: Sept 28 (416).

244A. Maeder, F.   1859: Feb 16 (139).

245. Mailet, Mlle.   1865: Mar 25 (304, 350).

246. Malvina, Anna 1847: Jy 28 (546), Aug 16 (638), 18 (638), 21 (638); 1852: Dec 15 (464), 16, 18 (86).

247. Manchester, Miss Jane 1851: May 31, Je 2.

248. Manchester, Miss Susan 1851: May 31, Je 2.

249. Marsh, Miss Mary 1853: Aug 15-20 (678), Aug 22-27 (678).

250. Marshall 1847: Jy 29 (406).

251. Marshals, Miss 1853: Jy 2+.

252. Moravia, Miss Blanche 1866: Nov 1+.

253. Martin, T. 1866: Nov 1+.

254. Mascret, Madame 1865: Mar 21 (345, 331), 25 (350).

255. Mathews 1853: Jy 2+, 28 #.

255A. Mattox 1859: Feb 16 (139).

256. Maxwell, G. H.   1866: Nov 1+.

257. Medina 1848: May 22 #.

258. Meeker, W. H.   1860: Nov 29 (140)**, Dec 19 (120), 21 (517), 22 (380), 24 (561, 149).

Meer. See Thorne and Mestayer.

259. Meldrum, R. S.   1858: Jy 17 (575); 1860: Mar 17 (565).

260. Melville, Miss   1865: Apr 21 (574).

260A. Menken, Miss Capt. Adah Isaacs   1859: Mar 14
    (204, 124).

Mestayer.   See Thorne and Mestayer.

261. Miller   1847: Apr 9+.

262. Millions   1850: Jy 10 (80).

263. Millon   1852: Oct 18 #.

264. Mitchel, Miss   1854: Jan 13 (406).

265. Mitchell, Miss   1852: Aug 14 (263), 21 (454), Sept
    23 (555), 25, Oct 19 #, 25 #, Nov 23, 27, Dec 22
    # (138); 1853: Jy 2+, 26 #.

266. Mitchell, Miss Emma   1860: Mar 17 (565).

267. Mitchell, Mrs. Emma   1853: Jy 2+.

268. Mitchell, Miss M. A.   1860: Mar 17 (565).

269. Mitchell, Maggie   1860: May 21, 22, 23 # (201, 569),
    26.

270. Mitchell, Miss Mary   1865: Dec 11 (573); 1867: Jan
    28- 29 (492), 30 (159, 750), 31 (447), Feb 1 (150),
    2 (563, 321).

271. Monett, Mrs.   1853: Oct 27 (339), 29 (438).

272. Monnell, Mrs.   1853: Jy 2+.

273. Moore   1852: Aug 16 #.

274. Moreton, Mrs. L.   1853: Oct 25 (253, 461); 1854:
    Jan 10 (371), 13 (380).

275. Morris, T.   1853: Oct 25 (253), 29 (438), Nov 3
    (335).

276. Morris, T. E.   1864: Dec 12- 14 (43).

277. Morton, John   1866: Nov 1+.

278. Moyn, L.   1853: Aug 22- 27 (678).

279. Murray, Master   1850: Je 19- 22.

280. Murray, Miss   1861: Sept 2 (107).

281. Myrick, M. H.   1853: Oct 25 (253, 461).

282. Myron, D.   1856: Jan 14-16 (8, 628), 17 (628, 8), 22 (8), 24 # (8).

283. Neafie, T. A. T.   1860: Jan 3 (229), 4- 5 (111), 6 (286), 7 (137), May 24 (229), 25 # (111, 49), 26; 1861: Sept 9 (229), 10 (111), 11 #, 12 (554); 1865: Feb 13 (385), 14 (286), 15 (111), 16 (229), 17 # (580, 18, 137), 18 (554, 49), Mar 20 (229), 21 (385), 22 (554), 23 (111), 24 # (111, 137), 25 (4, 49), Nov 6- 11 (229), 14 (286), 15 (632, 137), 16 (385), 17 (317); 1865: Nov 11 (229), 12 (286), 13 (317), 14 (4), 15 # (111), 16 (554).

284. Nelson, Miss   1854: Jan 21 (348).

285. Newkirk, Miss   1847: Jy 29 (120), Aug 14 (554).

286. Nickinson   1847: May 5 (430), 13 (339, 245), 17 # (569), Je 16 (80, 232), 18 (481), 24 (271), 30 # Jy 7 (431).

287. Nickinson, Miss Charlotte   1847: May 17, Je 16 (80, 232), 21 #, 28, Jy 3.

288. Northrop, Miss   1852: Nov 8 #.

289. O'Conner, J.   1852: Oct 20.

290. Owen, H. H.   1853: Oct 25 (253, 461), 27 (339), 29 (276).

291. Owen, J. E.   1867: Jan 14 (614, 405), 15 (614, 358), 16 # (503, 358), 17 (614, 661), 18 (686, 199), 19 (614, 661, 199).

292. Palmer, Jack   1865: Feb 10 (132).

293. Pardy, H. D.   1854: Jan 10 (371, 632), 11 (380), 12 (291, 635), 13 (380), 14- 16 (262), 17 (554), 20 (632, 635), 21 (301).

294. Parker, Mrs. Amelia   1854: Jan 2- 7 (678), 9 (678), 10 (371, 632), 11 (380), 12 (291, 635), 13 (380), 14- 16 (262), 17 (554), 20 (632, 635), 21 (301); 1855: Je 18- 20 (364), Dec 14 # (380, 371); 1857: Jan 22 (649), Feb 5 (262), 6 (592, 136), 18 (136), 19 # (74, 371, 727), 20 (74, 371, 727), Mar 2

(173)+; 1858: Jy 17 (575), 31 (486).

295. Parker, Ada 1847: Oct 4 (339), 7 (376).

296. Parker, Miss Jeanie 1864: Dec 1-3 (505), 5-7 (107), 12-14 (43).

297. Pearson, H. 1860: May 23 (201, 569), 26.

298. Pemberton 1852: Sept 23 (555).

299. Pentland, Miss 1849: Oct 15 (474).

300. Peters, Charles 1867: Jan 4 (458).

301. Phelps, A. R. 1847: Je 8 # (517).

302. Phillips, Daniel 1865: Mar 4 #.

303. Phillips, H. B. 1847: Je 3 (742), 4 # (222).

304. Phillips, N. 1851: May 31, Je 2.

305. Pike 1853: Oct 25 (253).

306. Pilgrim 1853: Jy 2+, Aug 1 #.

307. Pilgrim, J. 1853: Jy 2+; 1862: Apr 21.

308. Placide, Miss 1865: Nov 14 (286).

309. Plunkett, H. 1856: Jy 2 #, 5 (538), 7 (616, 398, 577).

310. Plunkett, Mrs. 1856: Jy 14 (292).

311. Plunkett, Miss Viola 1866: Nov 1+.

312. Ponisi 1861: Nov 7-9 (475), 11-14 (240).

313. Porten 1864: Sept 10 #, Oct 3 (146).

314. Porter, B. C. 1859: Oct 14-19 (678), 21-24 (678); 1864: Dec 16 (656).

315. Porter 1867: Sept 28 (385), Oct 25-26 (480).

316. Powers, Miss Julia 1859: Oct 14-19 (678), 21-24 (678); 1867: Sept 30 (253).

317. Pray, Miss 1850: Je 22 (141).

318. Price, Miss Fannie B. 1867: Oct 7-9 (470), 10 (170), 11 # (150), 12 (387).

319. Proctor, J. 1850: Nov 2 # (84, 467); 1851: Feb 20 (467, 698), 28 (541, 699), Mar 1 # (410, 24, 621); 1856: Jan 8 # (100).

320. Proctor, Mrs. J.   1851: Mar 1 (410, 621); 1856: Jan 8 (100).

321. Proctor, Joseph   1861: Dec 9-10 (467), 11-12 (209), 13 (436, 543), 14 (494, 543), 16 (385), 17 (494), 18 (14); 1867: May 13 (286), 14 (467), 15 (494), 16 (286), 17 # (467, 542), 18 (467, 542).

322. Provost, Miss Mary B.   1848: May 9 (715), 11 (486), 15.

323. Pryor, J. J.   1864: Sept 19 (678), 20-21.

324. Pyne, J. M.   1864: Oct 3 (106).

325. Randolph, Miss   1851: May 31, Je 2.

326. Ravel, Miss Marietta   1867: Nov 18-19 (204), 20 (731), 21 (708, 147), 22 # (201, 402).

327. Raymond, Malone   1857: Feb 6 (248).

328. Rea, Frank   1857: Mar 2 (508)+.

329. Rea, Mrs. Frank   1854: Nov 24; 1857: Mar 2 (173, 508)+.

330. Reed   1852: Aug 14 (263).

331. Reignolds, Kate   1867: May 6-7 (226), 8 (25), 9 (339, 22), 10 # (356, 556), 11 (25, 22).

332. Reignolds, The Misses   1861: Sept 2 (107).

333. Rice, T. D.   1847: Apr 14 (690), 15 (318), 16 (486), 17 (486, 192); 1849: Oct 26 (749, 690, 318), 27 (318, 192), 29 (485, 302), 30 (690, 485), 31 (318, 485), Nov 1 (192), 3 # (340, 689); 1850: Je 19-22; 1851: Feb 27 (442); 1852: Sept 9 (442), 30 (599), Oct 5 #, Nov 8.

334. Richardson, Miss Charlotte   1864: Oct 3 (146).

335. Riggins   1865: Apr 12 (77).

336. Roberts   1847: Je 16 (232).

337. Robertson, Miss   1867: Oct 7-9 (470).

337A. Robertson, Miss Angie   1859: Oct 14-19 (678), 21-24 (678).

338. Robinson, Frederick   1866: Jy 4 (552)**, (455)**.

339. Robson, Stuart   1866: Dec 24-27 (410, 189), 28 # (633), 29 (702), 31 (198, 326); 1867: Jan 2-3 (230,

310, 27), 4 # (488), 5 (288, 216).

340. Rodgers, Mrs. Howard 1861: Nov 2 (517), 7-9 (475), 12 (240), 14 (240), 18-19 (677).

341. Rodgers, J. H. 1861: Nov 2 (574), 11 (240), 13 (240).

342. Rogers 1861: Sept 2 (107).

343. Rose, Mrs. L. 1852: Oct 25 #.

343A. Rosene, C. 1859: Oct 14-19 (678), 21-24 (678).

344. Roseve 1867: Oct 25-26 (480).

345. Ross 1860: Mar 17 (565).

346. Rubahmah, Miss 1851: Jan 20 (55), 24 (55, 659), 25 (184), Feb 5 (169), 20 # (467, 698), 26 (502), 28 (698).

346A. Russell, H. 1859: Mar 14 (204).

347. Ryan 1849: Dec 17.

348. Ryan Children 1862: Mar 29 (678).

349. Ryan, D. 1860: Jan 4-5 (111), 6 (286), 7 (137, 467); 1861: Nov 11-14 (240), 18-19 (678).

350. Ryan, Kate Denin (see also Denin, Miss Kate) 1862: Mar 24 (240), 25 (488), 27 (316, 276), 28 #, 29 (678).

351. Ryan, Mr. Redmond 1849: Dec 18 (641); 1850: Je 19-22.

352. Ryan, Sam 1862: Mar 24 (34, 240), 25 (288), 27 (316, 276), 28 #, 29 (678); 1865: Jan 16 (437).

353. Sanford, E. 1857: Feb 17 (229), Mar 2 (173)+.

354. Saxon, Miss Kate 1857: Jan 22 (649, 608), Feb 5 (39), 6 # (592, 136), 17 (229, 752), 18 (136, 738), 19-20 (74), 21 (210, 668).

355. Scott, J. R. 1850: Je 8-9.

356. Scoville, Yankee 1854: Jan 27 (577, 717, 279).

357. Sefton, J. D. 1861: Sept 2, Nov 1 (722), 7-9 (475), 11-14 (240), 18-19 (678).

358. Seymore 1849: Oct 22 (481), 23 (125, 641, 714, 433), 24 (214, 648), 25 (49, 426, 654, 424).

359. Seymour, Mrs. 1799: Aug 7 (469, 425), 21 (210).

360. Seymour, Henry 1852: Aug 13 #.

361. Shields, G. W. 1866: Nov 1+.

362. Shields, W. D. 1866: Nov 8-10 (364), 19-22 (228).

363. Silsbee, J. S. 1847: Je 3 (742), 4 (15), 5 (737), 7 #(584, 313).

364. Sinclair, Mrs. 1850: Je 19-22.

365. Sinclair, Miss Annie 1850: Oct 26 (140, 307).

366. Sittell 1850: Jy 10 (138, 80).

367. Slate 1852: Nov 27.

368. Smith, A. 1847: Sept 6 (385).

369. Smith, C. J. 1847: Je 8 (517).

370. Smith, George 1856: Jy 14 (292).

371. Smith, J. S. 1859: 14-17 (8), 22 # (8), 24 (8).

372. Smith, Mark 1866: Jy 4 (552)** (455)**.

373. Somers, E. 1864: Oct 3 (106).

374. Spencer 1853: Aug 22-27 (678).

375. Sprague 1847: May 22 (82), Je 16 (232), 18 (481), 24 (148, 271), Aug 10 #.

376. Stafford 1847: Apr 9+.

377. Stanley, R. 1866: Nov 1+.

378. Stark 1847: Jy 27 (573), 28 (684), 30 # (120, 724), 31 (138, 165), Aug 2 (368), 4 (120), 5 (517), 9 (691, 283), Dec 24 (87).

379. Stephens, Miss 1853: Jy 2+.

380. Stetson, E. T. 1866: Feb 22 (400)*.

381. Stetson, Mrs. E. T. 1866: Feb (400)*.

381A. Stewart, J. L. 1859: Oct 14-19 (678), 21-24 (678).

382. Stone 1851: Feb 5 (169), 24-25 (530), Mar 1 (621).

383. Strong, J. B. 1847: Aug 20 (325), 21 (120), 23 (385), 25 (385), Oct 7 (276); 1853: Oct 25 (253), 27 (339), 28 (208), 29 (276), Nov 3 (335).

384. Strong, Mrs. J. B. 1853: Oct 25 (253), 27 (339), 28 (208), 29 (276), Nov 3 (335), 21 # (385).

385. Studley, J. B. 1860: Jan 2 (480), 4-5 (111), 6 (286), 7 (467).

386. Sullivan 1847: Apr 9+.

386A. Sylvester, Mrs. 1859: Feb 16 (139).

387. Sylvia, A. 1854: Jan 21 (348); 1859: Mar 14 (204); 1860: Jan 6 (286), 7 (467).

387A. Talma, Miss Adelaide 1859: Oct 14-19 (678), 21-24 (678).

388. Taylor, Miss 1853: Aug 22-27 (678).

389. Thomas 1860: Mar 17 (565).

389A. Thomaw, C. 1859: Oct 14-19 (678), 21-24 (678).

390. Thompson, Mrs. 1850: Jy 10 (138, 80).

391. Thompson, G. W. 1861: Nov 18-19 (678); 1862: Mar 14 (629, 27, 710).

392. Thompson, Mrs. G. W. 1862: Mar 3 (678).

393. Thorne and Mestayer, Messrs & Co. (Messrs. Lenox, Meer, Janvia, Chipp, Wray, Mesdames Thorne, Mestayer, Belcour & Miss Smith) 1832: May 8 (699, 623), 9 (632, 196), 11 (621, 687), 12 (667, 687, 546), 14 (120), 15 (280), 16 (554), 17 (517), 19 (486, 658, 564). See also Addams, A. A.

394. Thorpe 1852: Sept 23 (555).

395. Thorpe, Mrs. 1852: Sept 23 (555).

396. Tilton 1849: Oct 12 (355), 31 (632).

397. Tilton, E. L. 1861: Oct 31 (399), Nov 1 (341), 2 (517, 574), 7-9 (476), 11-14 (240), 18-19 (678).

398. Torry, Miss 1864: Nov 22 (165).

399. Turner 1853: Aug 22-27 (678); 1854: Feb 1 #.

400. Turner, J. B. 1856: 14-17 (8), 22 (8), 24 (8).

401. Tuttle, Miss 1857: Feb 21 (210).

402. Tyrell, George 1858: Jy 17 (575).

403. Vance, Tom 1863: Mar 4-6 (589), May 1 #.

404. Vanstavoren 1847: Apr 9+.

405. Varrey 1860: Jan 2 (480), 5, 6, (286, 598), 7 (137, 467, 598).

406. Vernon, Ida 1866: Je 11-12 (150).

407. Vincent, Felix 1865: Feb 27 (64, 297, 473), 28 (731, 608), Mar 1 (599), 2 (701, 360, 498), 3 (269).

408. Wall, H. 1860: Jan 4-5 (111), 6 (286, 598), 7 (137, 467).

409. Wallace, Miss C. J. 1864: Oct 3 (106).

410. Wallack, Miss Fanny 1850: Jy 15 (378, 165).

411. Wallack, J. W. 1847: May 18 (413), 19 (486), 20 (715, 444), 22 (245), 25 # (156, 3), 27 (684), 28 (156, 321), 29 (632, 736), Je 1 (229).

412. Wallack, J. W. Jr. 1861: Dec 24 (120), 26 (120).

413. Wallack, Mrs. J. W. Jr. 1861: Dec 24 (120), 26 (120).

414. Waller, D. S. 1866: Dec 6 (229), 8 (385)*, 12 (385), 12 (385), 13 (486), 14 (632), 15 (605), 29 (554); 1867: Apr 26 (486), 27 (621), May 20 # (253), Sept 28 (385), 30 (253), Oct 1-2 (145), Dec 1 (245, 125).

415. Waller, Mrs. Emma 1866: Nov 8-10 (364), 12 (632), 13 (253), 14 (339), 15 (245), 16 (588), 17 (303), 19-22 (228), 23 (74), 24 (380), Dec 8 (385)*, 10-11 (450), 12 (385), 13 (486), 14 (632), 15 (605), 1867: Feb 11-12 (228), 13-14 (696), Mar 18-22 (225), Apr 25 (228, 621), 26 (486), 27 (621), May 20 # (253, 508), Sept 28 (385), 30 (253), Oct 1-2 (145), 3 (228), Nov 25 (153), Dec 1 # (245, 125).

416. Wallis, Charles 1858: Jy 17 (276).

417. Walsh, J. C. 1866: Nov 1+.

418. Walters, Miss Clara 1860: Mar 22 (269, 278), 23
    (514), 24 (269, 415).

419. Ward, J. M. 1859: Feb 16 (139), Mar 5 (490),
    14 (204, 124), Ap 1 (140); 1864: Nov 28 (505, 351),
    Dec 1 (34), 2 (241), 5- 7 (107), 8 (267, 366), 9 #
    (656, 270); 1865: Jan 12 (577, 268, 454), Mar 6- 7
    505, 34), 8 (655, 270), 9 (270, 604), 10 # (107), 11
    (107), Apr 24 #, Jy 1 (680), 6 (186), 8 # (49), Dec
    25; 1866: May 17 (105, 366); 1867: Oct 25- 26 (480),
    28 (264, 34), 29 (269, 34), 30- 31 (365), Nov 1 #
    (161), 2 (365), 4 (505), 5 (161), 6 (107), 7 (505),
    8 # (322), 9 (322, 516).

420. Ward, W. M. 1861: Dec 19 (49), 21 (683), 23 (683,
    603).

421. Warwick 1866: Je 11 # (150), 12 (150).

422. Watts, Mrs. 1847: Apr 9+.

423. Weaver, John 1850: Oct 26 # (140, 307); 1852:
    Sept 23 (555).

424. Webb, Emma 1865: May (520, 504, 609), 2 (170),
    3 (520, 403), 4 (698, 106, 396), 5 (610, 735),
    6 (256, 211, 504).

425. Webb, Ida 1865: May 1 (520, 504, 609), 2 (170),
    3 (520, 403), 4 (698, 106, 396), 5 (610, 735),
    6 (256, 211, 504).

426. Wells, Louise 1862: Apr 21.

427. Wemyss, F. C. 1851: Feb 6- 8 (530), 10- 11 (412,
    54).

428. Wemyss, T. 1857: Feb 17 (229, 752), 18 (738),
    19- 20 (74), 21 (668), Mar 2 (508)+; 1859: Jan 1,
    Feb 16 (139).

429. Wentworth 1851: Feb 12.

430. Western, Miss Helen 1867: Mar 4 (188), 5 (204, 47),
    6 (204, 511), 7 (204, 137), 8 # (11, 554), 9 (111,
    415).

431. Western, Miss 1850: Je 22 (141, 198).

432. Western, Miss 1865: Feb 16 (229).

433. Western, Miss Mary 1864: Oct 3 (146); 1865: Mar 18.

434. Weymas, T. 1855: Je 18- 20 (364).

435. Wheeler, Miss   1847: May 17, Je 16 (232).

436. Whelpley, Isaac   1859: Apr 1 (140).

437. White, Cool   1862: Mar 3 (678)+, 21 #.

438. White, Mrs. Cool   1862: Mar 11 (570), 12.

439. Williams   1853: Oct 25 (253).

440. Williams, Mrs.   1853: Aug 22-27 (678).

441. Williams, Barney   1847: Je 28 (59), 29 (624, 37),
     30 (460), Jy 1 (276), 2 (355), 3 # (155, 277);
     1849: Oct 3 (276, 355), 5 (276, 232, 125), 6 (355,
     481), 8 (624, 232), 9 # (276, 37, 320, 214), 12
     (355), 16 (279, 320, 214), 17 (481, 214, 37), 18
     (59, 498, 434), 19 (624, 434, 273), 20 # (434, 499,
     642), Nov 21, 22 #; 1852: Oct 12, 13 (514), 15 #
     (16); 1867: Apr 1-2 (168), 3-4 (269, 261), 5 #-6
     (59, 577), 8-9 (574, 500), 10-11 (5, 110), 12 #
     (276, 278).

442. Williams, Mrs. Barney   1852: Oct 12, 13 (514), 15 #,
     16; 1867: Apr 1-2 (168, 118), 3-4 (269, 261),
     5 # (59, 577), 6 (59, 577), 8-9 (574, 500), 10 #-11
     (5, 100), 12 # (276, 278).

443. Williams, Miss Molly   1865: Feb 27 (64, 297, 473),
     28 (731, 608), Mar 1 (599), 2 (701, 360), 3 # (357,
     269).

443A. Willie, Master   1859: Oct 14-19 (678), 21-24 (678).

444. Wise   1852: Sept 23 (555).

445. Wise, E. S.   1860: Nov 29 (140)**.

446. Wood   1850: Jy 10 (138).

447. Wood, Miss Lizzie   1865: Jy 19 (412).

448. Woodward, Miss   1857: Feb 5 (39).

449. Woodward, Miss Joe   1864: Nov 12 (49).

450. Worchester   1861: Nov 7-9 (475), 11-14 (240).

451. Worrel Sisters   1866: Dec 17-18 (98, 449), 19 (266,
     114), 20, 21 #, 22.

     Wray.   See Thorne and Mestayer.

452. Wyette, Miss Charlotte 1852: Sept 23 (555), 24 (339), Oct 25 #, Dec 13 # (464, 177).

453. Young, A. W. 1866: Jy 4 (552, 455)**.
453A. Young, Mrs. E. W. 1859: Feb 16 (139).

454. Zoe, M'lle Marie 1866: Jan 22 (204).

Selective Bibliography

The major portion of the primary data collected for this study was derived from periodicals published in Newark during the period covered. The first newspaper was Woods's Newark Gazette, a weekly which began publication on May 19, 1791. With the November 8, 1797, issue it became simply the Newark Gazette and, as such, continued until December 25, 1804. The long-lived Centinel of Freedom began its weekly activities on October 5, 1796, with a continuous record until 1895. Its longevity is seconded by the Newark Daily Advertiser, which published daily, excluding Sunday, from March 1, 1832, to 1907. These publications cover and extend beyond the period of this study. Unlike the other publications, however, the Centinel of Freedom did not recognize on its pages the existence of theatrical activities. Thus, for the period from 1804 to 1832, the many short-lived publications, which also cover this period, were consulted in addition. For this rather extensive list, the reader is directed to the files of the New Jersey Historical Society and the Newark Free Public Library. Two other periodicals, however, should be cited for particularly good theater coverage: The Newark Daily Mercury, which published through much of the active period of this study, from January 13, 1849, to December 31, 1863, and the Temperance Advocate, which despite its name, gave critical support to the theater through much of 1847 and 1848.

178

From the rich and varied collections of the New Jersey Room of the Newark Free Public Library many items on the cultural, economic, and political life of the age can be found. Such basic materials as Pierson's Directory of the City of Newark (Newark: B. T. Pierson, 1836-67) and the various maps that graphically show the growth from town to city are frequently used references. There are three major histories of Newark. The earliest work is Joseph Atkinson's The History of Newark (Newark: William B. Guild, 1879) which is not really superseded by the 3 volume later work by Frank J. Urquhart, A History of the City of Newark, 1666 to 1913 (New York: Lewis Historical Publishing Co., 1913). Neither of them are concerned particularly with the amusement life of the city and the brief references to early theater (which Urquhart repeats in part from Atkinson) are largely informal and not documented. Both histories are oriented to the religious, economic, and political growth of the city. John T. Cunningham's Newark (Newark: The New Jersey Historical Society, 1966) was published after this work had been completed. Although he does not con-sider the theatrical life of Newark, I am including his book with recommendations. It is a highly readable volume, profusely illustrated, with much new material for the student of Newark and American history. Urquhart's A Short Histo-ry of Newark (Newark: Baker Printing Co., 1953), a re-issue with footnotes, and David Pierson's Narratives of Newark (Newark: Pierson Publishing Co., 1917) are shorter works which evoke a proud past, designed for popular reading.

Many of our early histories of the theater still re-main among our most valuable, particularly in those aspects which were contemporary with the author. This is true of William Dunlap's History of the American Theatre (New York: J. and J. Harper, 1832), Joseph N. Ireland's two volume work, Records of the New York Stage from 1750 to 1860 (New York: T. H. Morrell, 1866-67), and T. A. Brown's three volume work, A History of the New York Stage (New York: Dodd, Mead, 1903). Each of these works contains valuable items not found in the others. Nonetheless, in authority, all of these have been superseded by the most important of the local histories of the American theater, George C. D. Odell's fifteen volume Annals of the New York Stage (New York: Columbia University Press, 1927-49). Although overwhelming in their scholarship and often frustrating for the researcher, the Annals are fortunately not infrequently blessed by the good natured presence of their author.

Of other local histories, three individual works, which cover the Philadelphia theater from the eighteenth century to 1855, have particular pertinence. The first is T. C. Pollock's The Philadelphia Theatre in the Eighteenth Century (Philadelphia: University of Pennsylvania Press, 1933). It is followed in point of time covered by James D. Reed's Old Drury of Philadelphia, A History of the Philadelphia Stage, 1800-1835 (Philadelphia: University of Pennsylvania Press, 1932). The third work is A. H. Wilson's A History of the Philadelphia Theatre, 1835 to 1855 (Philadelphia: University of Pennsylvania Press, 1935). Together, these volumes are the authoritative record of the early Philadelphia theater. Unlike the Annals, however, they offer almost no narrative content. On the other hand, the theater researcher will find the various arrangements of data conveniently presented for his purposes.

The critical reminiscences of William Winter, The Wallet of Time, 2 vols. (New York: Moffat, Yard and Co., 1913), along with his other writings on plays and players, provide the researcher with an important body of primary materials. Similarly, Barnard Hewitt's Theatre U. S. A. 1668 to 1957 (New York: McGraw-Hill Book Co., 1959) is not only an interesting history of significant aspects of the American theater, but an excellent research source because of its use of extensive passages from contemporary accounts. Lloyd Morris' Curtain Time (New York: Random House, 1953), a highly readable informal history, provides many interesting stories. Both it and the encyclopedic work by Oral S. Coad and Edwin Mims, Jr., "The American Stage," vol. 14 of The Pageant of America (New Haven: Yale University Press, 1929) are profusely illustrated. A somewhat singular work is Alfred L. Bernhaim's The Business of the Theatre (New York: Benjamin Blom, Inc., 1964), an economic history of the theater, written at the request of Actors' Equity and originally published in twenty-one installments in Equity magazine.

The scholarship of many later students of the theater fortunately preserve for us much of the transitory, otherwise now lost, materials concerning our early theater. For the study of dramatic literature we are indebted to Arthur Hobson Quinn's A History of the American Drama from the Beginning to the Civil War (New York: F. S. Crofts, 1943). Foster Rhea Dulles' America Learns to Play (New York: D. Appleton-Century Company, 1940) affords us valuable insights into the amusements and social activities of early America.

Among the various theater periodicals, Theatre Annual and Theatre Survey contain many fine articles of value to the student of theater. The article by E. J. West, "Revolution in the American Theatre," Theatre Survey, I (1960), 43-64, is a very pleasant and rewarding experience, not generally the case for the researcher who continues to hunt for materials which he must frequently plow through, often only to discover that he cannot use them.